CROSS✦ROADS

Apostles' Creed

Author
Richard J. Reichert

BROWN-ROA

A Division of Harcourt Brace & Company

BROWN-ROA
A Division of Harcourt Brace & Company

O u r   M i s s i o n

The primary mission of BROWN-ROA is to provide the
Catholic and Christian educational markets with the
highest quality catechetical print and media resources.
The content of these resources reflects the best insights
of current theology, methodology, and pedagogical research.
The resources are practical and easy to use, designed to meet
expressed market needs, and written to reflect the
teachings of the Catholic Church.

Nihil Obstat
Rev. Richard L. Schaefer
Imprimatur
✠ Most Rev. Jerome Hanus, O.S.B.
Archbishop of Dubuque
January 4, 1998
Feast of Saint Elizabeth Ann Seton

The Imprimatur is an official declaration that a book or pamphlet is free of doctrinal or moral error. No
implication is contained therein that anyone who granted the Imprimatur agrees with the contents, opin-
ions, or statements expressed.

Illustrations: Rob Suggs
Photos Credits: Gene Plaisted, OSC/THE CROSIERS—iv, 21, 28, 31, 42, 47, 54, 61, 92, 99; Robert
Roethig—12, 93; James L. Shaffer—7, 17, 26, 37, 63, 69, 71; Skjold Photography—33, 49, 67, 81, 102,
106; Jim Whitmer—3, 9, 58, 65

Printed in the United States of America

ISBN 0-15-950470-8

10   9   8   7   6   5   4   3

Contents

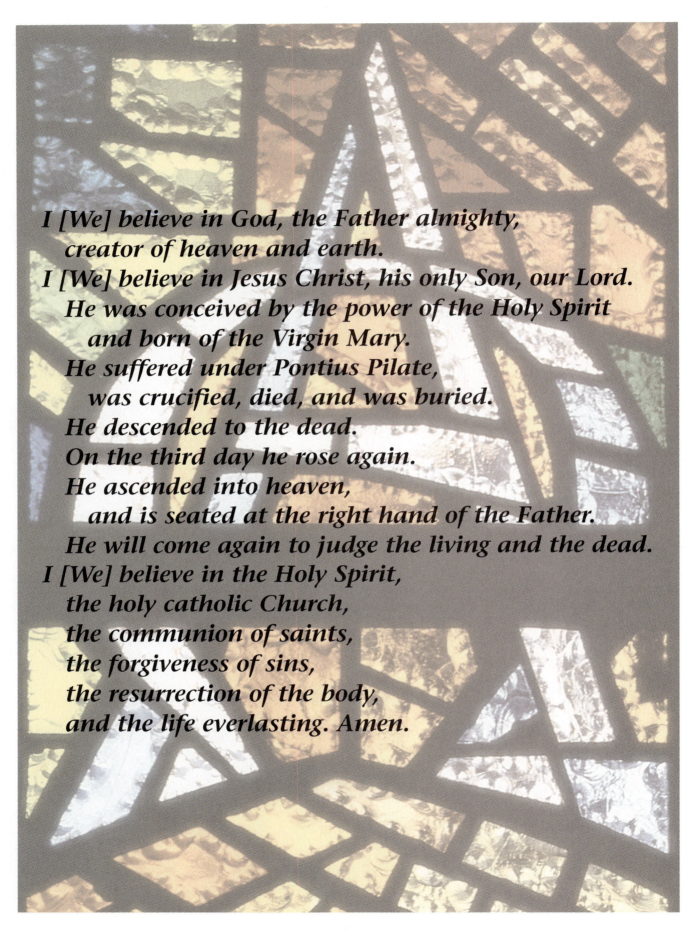

I [We] believe in God, the Father almighty,
  creator of heaven and earth.
I [We] believe in Jesus Christ, his only Son, our Lord.
  He was conceived by the power of the Holy Spirit
    and born of the Virgin Mary.
  He suffered under Pontius Pilate,
    was crucified, died, and was buried.
  He descended to the dead.
  On the third day he rose again.
  He ascended into heaven,
    and is seated at the right hand of the Father.
  He will come again to judge the living and the dead.
I [We] believe in the Holy Spirit,
  the holy catholic Church,
  the communion of saints,
  the forgiveness of sins,
  the resurrection of the body,
  and the life everlasting. Amen.

Chapter 1

THE GOD OF OUR ANCESTORS

I (we) believe in God, the Father almighty, creator of heaven and earth.

Setting the Stage: I Believe, I Believe . . .

If you believe something, you accept it as true or real, even though it may not be provable through scientific methods. What do you believe? Use these sentence starters to express your beliefs about the topics given. Then design a message or logo for a personalized T-shirt that communicates—in five words or less—an important belief you hold.

• About yourself

I believe _____

• About your family

I believe _____

• About your friends

I believe _____

• About school

I believe _____

• About nature

I believe _____

• About music

I believe _____

• About books

I believe _____

• About TV/video games

I believe _____

• About sports

I believe _____

• About life

I believe _____

Clearing the air

A whole course on the Apostles' Creed! You may be tempted to say, "You've got to be kidding!" or perhaps, "We know all that stuff already." Okay, those kinds of reactions are normal enough, but before you make up your mind that this course is going to be boring or a waste of time, let's see if we can clear the air a little.

We'll begin with a few facts about the Apostles' Creed. Did you know the apostles didn't write it? In fact, no one person or group wrote it. It developed in the Christian community at Rome in the second century as a kind of summary of the basic preaching of the apostles and first disciples, and it went like this:

I believe in God, Father almighty, and in Jesus Christ, his Son, our Lord, and in the Holy Spirit, the holy church, and the resurrection of the flesh.

Gradually, new generations of Christians expanded on these basic beliefs until the Creed reached its present form.

Catechism Corner

The Apostles' Creed is so called because it is rightly considered to be a faithful summary of the apostles' faith. . . . (194)

The Creed has survived as a summary of our faith for two reasons. First, it's short. Even a small child can learn it by heart. Second, it's simple and direct, listing all of our key beliefs in a very uncomplicated way. In fact, there was a time when studying the Apostles' Creed and the Lord's Prayer was *the* "religion course" used to teach both children and adults the basics of our faith. All the other aspects of the faith were learned more by experiencing and participating in the lived faith of a person's parish community.

What's Your View?

Form a group with two or three of your classmates. Share your responses to the following questions.

1. How do you participate in the lived faith of your parish community?
2. What have these experiences taught you?

But we still haven't answered the question of why you should take a whole course about the Creed. There are two main reasons. First, you have been attending religion classes for a number of years. You're ready to begin to put together all the pieces you've learned during that time. You're ready to form one clear, simple, and orderly picture of what often can seem like a lot of unrelated religious truths and facts. You're also becoming old enough to begin to *profess* and *live*, not simply know about, your faith. A study of the Apostles' Creed at this point in your growth can be a big help in moving from "knowing about" to "believing and living" your faith.

POST-IT QUOTE

Out of our beliefs are born deeds; out of our deeds we form habits; out of habits grows our character; and on our character we build our destiny.
Henry Hancock

ON YOUR OWN
Just DO It

A wise person once noted that "people will seldom believe what you say, but they will always believe what you do." Translating your religious beliefs and values into action is the best way of showing others how meaningful these beliefs and values are to you. In other words, "Just DO it!"

How do you live your faith at home? At school? In your neighborhood? In your parish community? Jot down your ideas here.

_____

_____

_____

_____

_____

_____

Catechism Corner

Believing is possible only by grace and the interior helps of the Holy Spirit. But it is no less true that believing is an authentically human act. . . . (154)

The second reason for studying the Creed now is that some young people, for one reason or another, haven't been attending religion classes regularly up to now. If that is your case, then a careful study of the Apostles' Creed is a quick way to catch up on what you've been missing.

So it makes no difference if you've been studying your faith regularly for a number of years or if you're just getting started. A study of the Apostles' Creed is going to be very useful to you. By the time you're finished with the course, you'll have a solid grasp of the core message of your faith. This message never changes, and as you'll see in a minute, it gives you a map you can follow all your life.

Journey Within

Think about what you have learned in your religious education classes and what you have experienced in the faith life of your parish. Write a paragraph expressing what you believe is the core message of your faith.

_____

_____

_____

All we can ask is that you be open-minded and give us a chance. We're convinced this course can be both useful and enjoyable for you.

3

In the space below, draw a simple map of a route with which you are very familiar. Here are some suggestions:

• from your house to your best friend's house

• from your house to a grandparent's house

• from one room in your school to another

• from one store at the mall to another

• from your house to your school

• from one part of a campground to another

Highlight your departure and destination points, and include directions, distances, landmarks, and points of interest.

Share your map with a partner or a small group of your classmates. How reliable is your map?

Map-Making

When the famous explorers Lewis and Clark set out to investigate the lands west of the Mississippi River in 1804, all they had to guide them were little bits and pieces of information gathered from previous explorers. They had no real facts about how big the territory was, what people might be living there, what rivers and mountains marked the landscape, and what kinds of animals and plants they might find.

When their trip was over, Lewis and Clark had a clear, detailed map of the territory. From then on, their map became the *creed* for anyone wanting to journey into that wilderness. Future travelers put their faith in that map to guide them. They believed in the map. Because they did, they were able to avoid many mistakes and dangers. They were able to reach their destination directly without first having to wander around, trying to find their way.

When you think of it, you are now a traveler yourself. You have started out on the most important journey of all: the journey through life. Like any traveler, you have questions. What lies ahead? What's the best route to take to reach my goal? What are the dangers and false trails I should avoid?

Journey Within

Jot down ten important questions you have about your life journey. Draw an asterisk in front of the three questions you consider the most significant.

_____

_____

_____

_____

_____

Your ancestors in faith have made the journey before you. In the process, they developed a "map of life" for you. It gives all the key landmarks you'll need to guide you. It tells you all you need to know to make the journey safely. You simply have to put your trust in your ancestors and believe in the map they gave you. Of course, the map we're speaking of is the Apostles' Creed.

Filling in the details

A map like the one Lewis and Clark developed gives you the unchanging basics. The mountains and rivers they discovered are still where they said they were. The distance from one place to another is still the same. So in a sense, a good map doesn't change.

But a map can't give information about some of the things that do change, such as how beautiful the mountains look in spring or how deep the snow can get in winter. A map can't tell you the best clothes to wear when you're traveling at a particular time of year.

In other words, a map is a guide. It gives you all the basics you need to know. But it's still up to you to use common sense in figuring out some things for yourself. For example, if you plan to travel in winter you'd better take some warm clothes. Also, many people who traveled through that territory later wrote diaries, journals, and stories that added a lot of information the original map didn't include, such as how high the snow gets in the mountains in the winter or the best place to cross a river in the spring.

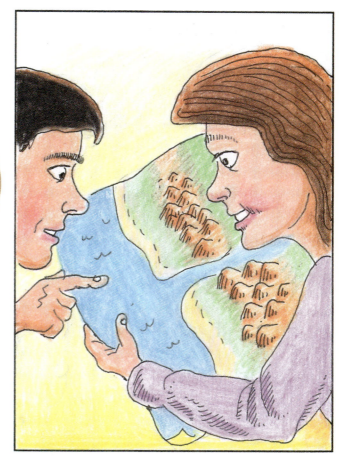

Revisit the map you drew earlier. What details might you add to make it better? On the lines below, list several "advisory notes"—things travelers should know about the route you mapped in order to make their journey as pleasant and trouble-free as possible.

1. _____
2. _____
3. _____
4. _____
5. _____
6. _____

It's the same with the "map of life" your ancestors in faith gave you. The Apostles' Creed contains all the basic truths you need as you journey through life, but you still have to use common sense and good judgment in making practical, day-to-day decisions.

POST-IT QUOTE

Life is not a spectator sport.

Obviously, these basic truths don't change, but others who have already made the journey of life by following the Apostles' Creed (the members of the Church over the centuries) have been able to add important details about our faith that the Apostles' Creed doesn't spell out. They offer a detailed understanding of the relationship between God the Father, Jesus, and the Holy Spirit. They give details on the nature of the Church itself and its sacraments. They provide details about Mary, the mother of Jesus, and her important helping role in our journey. They give us details about the Bible as God's special revelation to us.

What's Your View?

Get together with a partner. Share your ideas about how the Apostles' Creed is like a map.

So in one sense, it's true that all you need to know about our Catholic faith is contained in the Apostles' Creed. To use it well as a guide for your journey through life, you'll still have to make day-to-day decisions, and you'll need to learn the important details the Church has been able to fill in over the centuries as it followed this map through life.

The God question

Contrary to what many people think, the "God question" doesn't ask, "Is there a God?" To the question "Is there a God?" most humans in every age have said, "Yes!" The majority of people in every age have had no trouble realizing there is some Divine Being that is the controlling force in the universe. So the real God question is this: "Who is God to you?"

POST-IT QUOTE

We trust not because "a God" exists, but because "this God" exists.

C.S. Lewis

Form a group with two or three of your classmates. Share your responses to the following questions.

1. How did you picture God when you were four or five years old? How do you picture God now?

2. Have your perceptions changed? If so, why? If not, why not?

Over the centuries, people have come up with many different answers to that question. For a long time, most people thought there were a lot of competing gods—some friendly, some evil. For example, in these early times many people thought each object and force in the natural world—the wind, the sun, an animal, a tree—had its own divine spirit. The different kinds of religions that developed depended on how different societies understood their god or gods. If a group of people believed their god was a cruel, warrior-god, they might think it would be a religious act to sacrifice captured enemies to their god to keep it happy. If a group worshiped a food-giving farmer-god, their religion might center around planting and harvesting feasts.

 Breakaway

Seek and Search

In pairs or small groups, research the background on one of the gods listed below. Report to your class on what religion honored this god and what kind of actions were performed to offer worship to this god.

Allah

Apollo

Cupid

Diana

Dionysus

El Shaddai

Great Spirit

Kali

Shiva

Vulcan

Zeus

So the answer to the question "Who is God to you?" is very basic. It's what determines the kind of religion that will make sense to you. It determines what you consider good and evil acts, what is really important in life—and what life is actually all about. That's why, in the journey through life, answering the question "Who is God to you?" is the starting point. It sets you off in a particular direction. If you don't try to answer the question, or if you don't even bother to ask it, you never really get started. You wander around in life without any real purpose or direction.

Journey Within

In twenty-five words or fewer, answer the God question: "Who is God to you?"

_____

_____

_____

_____

_____

Breakaway
Perfect Parents

With a small group of your classmates, brainstorm a list of several qualities a perfect parent would possess. Contribute your group's ideas to a banner or poster produced by the entire class entitled "Perfect Parents." Post the banner in your classroom.

According to our map. . .

Remember, when our ancestors developed our Creed they put down only the most basic truths. So how they answered the question "Who is God?" is very important to us. Of all the things they could have said, the very first thing they did say is, "We believe in God the Father." In our ancestors' view, the most important thing you need to understand about God as you travel through life is that God is like a loving, concerned parent and

that you are God's beloved child. They are stressing that the most important thing you need to know about God is that he is personally concerned about you, your safety, and your happiness.

You've probably grown up hearing those kinds of words all your life. But now you're old enough to let them really sink in. Be careful that you don't just mouth them without really thinking about them. In short, do you really believe your God is a loving God who cares for you very personally?

Journey Within

How has God shown that he cares about you, your safety, and your happiness?

_____

_____

_____

_____

Before we say any more, here's an important thing to remember. Whatever words or statements we use to describe God usually have an unwritten "kind of like" in front of them. We can't define God the way we can define creatures. We always have to talk about our invisible, unlimited God by making comparisons to the limited things we do see and know.

So to say that God is "Father" means that our God is kind of like a good father or mother or has all of the best qualities all good fathers and mothers possess. On the other hand, because God is only "kind of like" the human parents we see, our God does not have any of the weaknesses and shortcomings we find in human parents.

Catechism Corner

. . . [God] is neither man nor woman. . . . But the respective "perfections" of man and woman reflect something of the infinite perfection of God: those of a mother and those of a father and husband. (Cf. *Isa* 49:14–15; 66:13; *Ps* 131:2–3; *Hos* 11:1–4; *Jer* 3:4–19.) (370)

What's Your View? 👁

Form a group with two or three of your classmates. Share your responses to the following questions.

1. In what ways is God like a perfect parent?
2. What human weaknesses or shortcomings do parents possess?
3. Why is it important for you—a daughter or son—to know that parents have weaknesses and shortcomings?

As we said, to our ancestors the most important truth about God is that our God is a loving, caring God who brought you into life, who always remains close to you, and is always concerned about you. They could have talked first about God as Judge, Lord, Master, or any of several other things. But they didn't. God is Father: that is the single most important thing you need to believe about God, according to our ancestors in faith.

Everything else about our Catholic religion and all the decisions you'll have to make as you journey through life need to be looked at in the light of that most fundamental of all truths: Your God is a Father who loves you always and desires your happiness always.

All other people are God's children, too—your brothers and sisters. Our loving God expects us to care for and treat each other that way!

Almighty God

Of course, God is almighty, the one all-powerful, all-knowing God, in total control of all that is in the universe. Our ancestors aren't primarily trying to say anything new here. But when you start out by believing God is a loving, caring Father, it means God uses this almightiness for your good and your protection. God loves you with an almighty love! Nothing or no one that exists can prevent God from loving and caring for you.

Catechism Corner

. . . Nothing is impossible with God, who disposes his works according to his will. (Cf. *Jer* 27:5; 32:17; *Lk* 1:37.) He is the Lord of the universe, whose order he established and which remains wholly subject to him and at his disposal. . . . (269)

Scripture Search

Read Romans 8:31. In your own words, restate Paul's message.

_____

_____

_____

_____

 Breakaway

"Oh, God(dess)!"

Ancient Greek society worshiped many gods and goddesses, several of whom are named below. Draw a symbol representing each of the figures named. Which god or goddess would be your favorite? Explain your answer.

Ares (god of war)

Demeter (goddess of agriculture)

Iris (goddess of the rainbow)

Aphrodite (goddess of love)

Poseidon (god of the sea)

Helios (god of the sun)

Hera (goddess of marriage, women, and childbirth)

Artemis (goddess of the hunt)

Nike (winged goddess of victory)

My favorite: _____

At the same time, by stressing that our God is almighty, our Creed is correcting a common mistake many earlier religions made. Most other religions at the time of our first Christian ancestors professed that there were many different gods, each with a particular power or area of control in the universe. Our ancestors stressed that there is only one God who is in total control of all that is.

You probably take this for granted. It's what you've always believed. But just a few thousand years ago, you'd have been very much in the minority. Even today, you might be surprised to find out how many people in various parts of the world still follow religions that talk about many different gods or spirits, each with its own particular powers.

What our ancestors are telling us is this: There is only one, almighty God. But our God does not use this divine almightiness to frighten, control, or enslave. Our God uses the divine almightiness to care for, protect, and save us, his beloved children. That is important to think about as you prepare to go out to face the world on your own.

Creator of heaven and earth

When our ancestors tell us our God is the Creator-God, they are emphasizing one particular part of God's almightiness. Most ancient and not-so-ancient religions thought the stuff out of which our universe is made was always here, along with the various gods. It was the gods' job to shape it and try to control its forces.

Catechism Corner

We believe that God needs no pre-existent thing or any help in order to create . . . God creates freely "out of nothing." (Lateran Council IV [1215]: DS 800; cf. DS 3025.) (296)

Our ancestors, on the other hand, starting way back with the Hebrews, have always believed that not one single atom existed until God willed it into existence; not one single atom can continue to exist unless God wills it so.

What's Your View?

Get together with a partner. Share your ideas about why our ancestors in faith stressed God's almightiness and how God uses his divine almightiness.

Scripture Search

Read the creation story as told in the first chapter of Genesis. As you read, make a list of what God created on each "day." How does this story emphasize that humans are the pinnacle, or high point, of God's creation?

ON YOUR OWN

Pass It On

God has chosen you to "pass on" the good news of his love and concern for his people. Write a brief note to a friend or family member. In your note, tell the person about God's loving concern for him or her. Be sure to deliver the message, or leave it in a place where the person will find it. (For a real surprise, sign your note "Love, God"!)

As you get older, you're going to learn more and more about what modern science tells us about the universe. But here's something to keep in mind as you do. Even our most advanced scientists have to admit that the more they learn about our universe, the more they end up facing mystery. Science can't tell us where the universe with all its marvelous laws and forces—especially life itself—came from in the first place. For that you need the help of the Holy Spirit. Only through faith, a gift from God, can we believe in the unexplainable.

So when you are able to say with real conviction that you believe in God, the Creator of heaven and earth, you have a head start on some of the most learned people in the world today. Those are not just pious words. They are profound truths.

Journey Within

When you say you believe in God, the Creator of heaven and earth, what do you mean?

_____

_____

_____

_____

There's another very important truth that goes along with this belief that our Creator started out with nothing and called all that is into existence. Everything has God's fingerprints on it! Everything can tell you something about the Creator. So even if you can't see God directly, everywhere you look you can learn something about God's wisdom, beauty, power, and gentleness.

You can look at a sunset and say, "God must be kind of like that." You can also look at a tiny baby or a huge whale, a butterfly or a tree branch, a grain of sand or a whole galaxy, and say, "God must be kind of like that." Perhaps most important, you are one of God's children, God's special work of creation. In a special way, you—and every human—have been made in God's image, a reflection of the Creator.

Scripture Search 📖

Locate and read Psalm 8:2, 4–10. Rewrite the psalmist's message in modern-day language.

_____

_____

_____

What's Your View? 👁

Get together with a partner. Tell him or her about some of the things in creation that most help you "see" God.

Breakaway
God's Fingerprints

Everything that exists tells us something about the God who created it. Brainstorm words or phrases beginning with each of the letters below that identify or describe elements of creation that bear God's fingerprints. When you are finished, you will have created an acrostic poem to share with your classmates. You might also want to illustrate your work with pictures clipped from used magazines.

G _____

O _____

D _____

'S _____

F _____

I _____

N _____

G _____

E _____

R _____

P _____

R _____

I _____

N _____

T _____

S _____

God is always Creator. God didn't simply create the universe and then move off to some distant heaven to observe it from afar.

Catechism Corner

. . . God does not abandon his creatures to themselves. He not only gives them being and existence, but also, and at every moment, upholds and sustains them in being . . . (301)

God remains present and involved in the universe, holding it in existence, caring for it, and guiding it to its final end. One important way God does this is by calling on us to share in this work of creation. In a real sense, God has formed a partnership with humans in caring for and continuing the work of creation. He calls on us to be good stewards of all creation. God asks us to use our gifts and talents to make the world more beautiful.

ON YOUR OWN
Creator at Work

Think about your activities of the past week. What have you done to care for and continue the work of creation? Jot down some of your ideas on an index card or small piece of paper. Your teacher will collect the cards, which will be used during the "Prayer for Today" that concludes this chapter.

Two kinds of faith

There are actually two ways to talk about faith. Faith is a way of knowing another person. Faith is also a way of knowing what is truth. The two kinds of faith are closely connected. The first kind of faith means that you *believe in* that person. The second kind of faith, as a way of knowing the truth, means you *believe that* something is true even if you can't prove it.

Journey Within

Tell about a person you know (family member, teacher, or friend, for example) who is very special to you—someone you believe in. What makes this person worthy of your believing in her or him?

_____

_____

When you have faith in or you believe in another person, it basically means you have become convinced the other is so good that you are able to entrust your whole self to that person—your life, your possessions, your secrets, your whole future. Small children believe in their parents this way. Close friends believe in each other this way. This kind of belief in each other is what holds two people together in marriage. Faith as a way of knowing another person is very close to what we usually mean when we say we love someone. Faith is knowing another person with your heart and not just your head.

ON YOUR OWN
A Work of Heart

Create a homemade "work of heart"—a special kind of valentine—to give to someone you believe in. On your valentine, tell the person why you believe in her or him. Don't wait until Valentine's Day to send it—the person will enjoy receiving it now!

If you believe in someone in this complete kind of way, it follows that you'll believe the things that he or she tells you, even if you can't prove it yourself. For example, you have a really good friend, someone you believe in. She's also a great blader. If she tells you Brand X in-line skates are the best kind for you to buy, you'll take her word for it. You don't ask for more proof. You wouldn't be so quick to believe it if a salesperson you don't know said it. You'd want more proof.

Religious faith is like that. It means believing in God. It also means believing the things God tells us even when we can't prove them directly.

POST-IT QUOTE

There are no tricks in plain and simple faith.
William Shakespeare

Our religious faith is much more than simply believing that God exists or that God is all-powerful and so forth. It means we really entrust our whole self to God the way small children entrust themselves to a loving parent, or a husband and wife entrust themselves to each other, or as you trust your best friend. To have religious faith—to have faith in God—means to be "best friends" with God. It is much more than accepting some ideas about God or religion. It means knowing God with your heart. This kind of faith is a gift from God accepted through the help of the Holy Spirit.

Religious faith also involves believing in other believers, those who have arrived at this kind of faith in God before us. And it means believing the things these more experienced believers—people who know God with their hearts—tell us about God. For most of us, this means first of all believing in our parents and other older relatives, such as grandparents, aunts, and uncles. It also means believing in our religion teachers, our pastor, and the other official leaders of the Church, such as the bishops and the pope. It means believing in our ancestors in faith.

ON YOUR OWN

Best Friends with God

Knowing God with your heart means that you are best friends with him. In the heart drawing below, list several ways you can be a best friend to God.

Catechism Corner

. . . The believer has received faith from others and should hand it on to others. Our love for Jesus and for our neighbor impels us to speak to others about our faith. Each believer is thus a link in the great chain of believers. . . . (166)

So when you read or recite the Apostles' Creed, you are dealing with both kinds of faith. It is a summary of truths you can't really prove. You believe *that* all God has revealed is true. The reason you have this kind of faith is because you have the other kind of faith: you have faith *in* God and *in* the people who are telling these truths to you. When you pray the Creed, you are expressing both kinds of faith.

Reflection

O LORD, our Sovereign,
    how majestic is your name in all the earth!
You have set your glory above the heavens.
    Out of the mouths of babes and infants
you have founded a bulwark because of your foes,
    to silence the enemy and the avenger.
When I look at your heavens, the work of your
    fingers,
        the moon and the stars that you have
        established;
what are human beings that you are mindful of
    them,
        mortals that you care for them?

Yet you have made them a little lower than God,
    and crowned them with glory and honor.
You have given them dominion over the works of
    your hands;
        you have put all things under their feet,
all sheep and oxen,
    and also the beasts of the field,
the birds of the air, and the fish of the sea,
    whatever passes along the paths of the seas.
O LORD, our Sovereign,
    how majestic is your name in all the earth!
                                        —Psalm 8

Prayer for Today

Side One: O almighty God and Father,

The wonders of your universe fill us with awe.

Side Two: All of creation was called into being at your will,

from distant galaxies—vast beyond imagination—

to the tiniest grain of sand on the shore.

Side One: Thank you for calling us to life,

for creating us in your image,

for loving us beyond measure,

and for gifting us with the beauty and majesty around us.

Side Two: Keep us mindful of our responsibilities as caretakers of the earth,

so that all who come after us can be touched by your goodness.

Side One: Lead us gently to eternal life with you.

All: Amen.

HOMEWORK

The first words of the Apostles' Creed emphasize three of our beliefs about God: that he is almighty; that he loves us in much the same way as a father or mother loves his or her child; and that he called into existence and sustains all of creation. In the space below, create one symbol for God that illustrates these three godly characteristics.

FATHER   **ALMIGHTY**   **CREATOR**

Chapter 2

DISCIPLES OF JESUS

. . . and in Jesus Christ, His only Son, our Lord.

Setting the Stage: Fan-ship or Friendship?

How is *being a fan of* someone different from *being friends* with someone? Get together with a small group of your classmates to share your ideas.

This year's superstars

A few years ago, when a certain rock superstar came to a big city to perform in concert, people began camping outside the arena two days ahead of time to be sure they would get tickets. The next year, when that same star came to the city for a concert, hardly anyone showed up. Popularity is like that in the entertainment world. Stars rise and fall all the time. This year's superstar is often next year's has-been. Fans may be totally dedicated for a time. They buy every CD, poster, and T-shirt they can find while the star is hot. But they tend to have short memories.

POST-IT QUOTE

Fame is chiefly a matter of dying at the right time.

What's Your View?

With a small group of your classmates, share your ideas in response to the following questions.

1. Name five superstars from the world of music, movies, TV, sports, or fashion who currently have millions of fans. Which (if any) of these superstars was as popular three years ago as now?

2. Name five celebrities from the world of music, movies, TV, sports, or fashion who had millions of fans in the past but are no longer considered "superstars." What caused these stars to fade?

3. Do you think a person who has millions of fans still needs friends? Explain your answer.

Why do you think this happens? There are a lot of possible reasons, of course, but the core reason seems to be this: Being *fans* isn't the same as being *friends*. As a fan, you have to follow from afar. Even if you get to attend a live concert and sit in the front row, there is usually a wall of burly security guards between the star and you, the fan. What you know about the star comes from news stories, not from personal contact. Let's face it: it's hard to keep up a long-term relationship with someone who doesn't even know you exist.

Friends, on the other hand, like to be together. You and your friends know each other "up-close and personal." You and your friends share all kinds of day-to-day interests and concerns. You and your friends care for each other in very practical ways. That's why friendships can last a lifetime.

ON YOUR OWN

Up-Close and Personal

Interview a good friend and then write a short biography about him or her. Give the biography to your friend as a special gift.

I believe in Jesus . . .

Jesus isn't like some superstar who was popular with his fans for a few years a long time ago and then lost his popularity. It's true that Jesus did have a group of dedicated followers way back during his time on earth two thousand years ago. But Jesus still has dedicated followers today, twenty centuries later—millions of them. The reason is that Jesus invited all those who first approached him to become his friends, to enter into a close, personal friendship with him. Jesus didn't remain at a safe distance, aloof, protected by security guards or his divine powers. He liked to be with his followers.

Catechism Corner

From the beginning of his public life Jesus chose certain men, twelve in number, to be with him and to participate in his mission. . . . (Cf. *Mk* 3:13–19.) (551) Christ invites his disciples to follow him by taking up their cross in their turn. . . . (Cf. *Mt* 10:38.) (1506)

Scripture Search

Jesus' apostles and some of his disciples were his closest friends. Read the Bible passages listed below to find the answers to some questions about Jesus and his relationship with his friends.

1. Whom did Jesus call to be his apostles? (Matthew 10:2–4 and Luke 6:12–16)

2. What qualities did Jesus look for in a friend? (Mark 1:14–20)

3. What did Jesus expect his friends to do? (Luke 5:1–11, 9:23–25; Mark 6:12–13)

4. How did Jesus show his friendship to his disciples in Luke 8:22–25?

5. How did Jesus show a special love for his friend Lazarus? (John 11:1–43)

And it's still the same today. Jesus wants to be friends with all who approach him now. Jesus enjoys and wants to share, to help, to be with people like you and me. It's been that way in each generation for two thousand years. That's one of the reasons Jesus' popularity hasn't faded.

What's Your View?

Get together with a partner and share your ideas about why Jesus is as popular today as he was during his earthly life.

When our ancestors developed the Creed, of all the things they could have said about Jesus, the very first thing they tell us is simply to believe in Jesus. They didn't first list a lot of abstract truths. The Creed simply points us to Jesus—this Son of God and son of Mary—and says, "Trust him to be your friend. Believe in him."

Journey Within

If Jesus were to come to your town and stay at your home as a guest, where would you invite him to go? If he wanted to be around lots of people, where would you suggest he go? Where would you take him if he wanted to teach? What would the two of you do for entertainment? Where would you take him for a good meal? Where would you suggest he go if he wanted to be alone with his thoughts?

_____

_____

_____

_____

_____

POST-IT QUOTE ☑

Thus says the Lord, . . . I have called you by name, you are mine.

Isaiah 43:1

Catechism Corner

Jesus means in Hebrew: "God saves." At the annunciation, the angel Gabriel gave him the name Jesus as his proper name, which expresses both his identity and his mission. . . . (Cf. *Lk* 1:31.) (430)

What's in a Name?

In the famous balcony scene from Shakespeare's Romeo and Juliet, Juliet muses, "What's in a name?" Look up the meaning of your given (first) name. Find out from your parent(s) why you were given this name. If you could choose your own name, what name would you select? Why?

Who do you say I am?

You've heard the words *Jesus Christ* used together so often you may think that "Christ" is Jesus' family name, just as John Smith's family name is Smith. But "Christ" is actually a title of Jesus, not his family name. The real way to say it is like this: Jesus, the Christ. The title *Christ* means "the Anointed One of God." The Hebrew word for "the Christ" is *Messiah*. So to say "Jesus Christ" is actually to say "Jesus, the Christ, the Anointed One, the Messiah." That's what it means in our Creed, too. Our ancestors are telling us to believe that this Jesus is the very Messiah promised by God to the Jewish people.

Scripture Search

Read the following Scripture passages to discover some other names Jesus is known by.

Matthew 16:16   _ _ _ / _ _ / _ _ _ / _ _ _ _ _ _ / _ _ _

Matthew 21:9   _ _ _ / _ _ / _ _ _ _ _ _

Luke 5:12   _ _ _ _

Luke 22:48   _ _ _ / _ _ / _ _ _

John 1:29   _ _ _ _ / _ _ / _ _ _

John 11:28   _ _ _ _ _ _ _

John 12:13   _ _ _ _ / _ _ / _ _ _ _ _ _

The Hebrew Scriptures (Old Testament) tell us about this promised Messiah and how he would lead all people back into friendship with God. Our first ancestors in faith were Jews, children of Abraham. Our ancestors were not expecting the Son of God, but a messiah, someone who would free them from slavery and again make their nation great over all other nations. Only after the resurrection did Jesus' followers begin to understand the kind of messiah God had sent. Those who followed Jesus began to be called *Christians* precisely because they believed Jesus was the Messiah, the one, true Christ, the Savior promised by God.

People considered these first Christians dangerous, a threat to the government and to both the Jewish religion and the established religions of the time. In those first days, those words of the Creed weren't some empty formula to repeat without thinking. To say you believed that Jesus is the only Son of God was enough to get you arrested, even killed.

Journey Within

Reflect on what it means to you to be a Christian.

Breakaway

Christian on Board

Many people purchase vanity plates for their automobiles: special, customized license plates that reveal their hobby, occupation, or some other interesting aspect of their identity. Design a vanity plate for a true follower of Christ, using letters, numbers, and symbols. Share your finished plate with the class.

What's Your View?

Get together with a partner to solve this riddle: Two fathers and their two sons went fishing. Their luck was bad; they caught only three fish. But they managed to divide the fish equally among them without cutting or splitting any of the fish! How was that possible?

The only Son of God

When our ancestors placed the words "his only son" in the Creed, they expressed what is at the heart of being Christian. They are saying that this man Jesus is not just the promised Christ, but that he is God's divine Son. These words say Jesus shares his divine nature with God the Father—completely. Jesus has all the same divine qualities and powers of God the Father. In short, Jesus is the Son of God!

We are at the heart of a great mystery here. (The official word for it is the *incarnation*. We'll explore this mystery further in the next chapter.) In the Creed, our ancestors don't attempt to explain how it is possible for Jesus to be both fully human and fully God. They don't attempt to explain why, if Jesus and the Father are both God, we don't have two Gods. They don't attempt to prove any of this in the Creed. That isn't what creeds do. The Creed simply says that what we believe is true and that to be a Christian means to believe that Jesus of Nazareth is God, the only Son of God the Father.

POST-IT QUOTE

No one is a martyr for a conclusion; no one is a martyr for an opinion; it is faith that makes martyrs.
John Henry Newman

But that didn't stop our ancestors from believing and from trying to help others to come to believe in Jesus, too. So we really have to admire those first Christians, our ancestors in faith. They were true pioneers: trailblazers who were willing to risk their lives for their belief that Jesus is the only Son of God. This same belief is the foundation for all the core beliefs we hold as Jesus' disciples today—Jesus, totally divine, totally human, is the source of all truth and the Savior of the world.

What's Your View?

Form a group with two or three of your classmates. Share your responses to the following questions.

1. In your opinion, is being a Christian in today's world as dangerous as it was to be an early Christian? Explain your answer.

2. Your text compares early Christians to "trailblazers." What are some personal characteristics of trailblazers?

3. True followers of Jesus Christ continue to blaze trails today. Who are some modern Christian trailblazers whom you admire?

ON YOUR OWN

The Ultimate Test of Faith

Read about the life of an early Christian martyr (Saint Stephen or Saint Agnes, for example) or about a twentieth-century martyr (Saint Edith Stein or Saint Maximillian Kolbe, for example). Share what you learn with the class.

Saint Joan of Arc

Our Lord

If it is now easy for you to believe that Jesus is God's only Son, you have your ancestors in faith to thank for it. Just be careful that it doesn't become too easy for you. Don't fall into the trap of taking your faith in Jesus for granted. As you continue to grow, keep coming back to those words in the Creed. Let them sink deep inside you. Your friend, Jesus, is the Son of God.

If the words "his only son" become living words for you, then the words "our Lord," which follow, take on the meaning the Creed intends them to have. When our ancestors included the words "our Lord" in describing their faith in Jesus, they moved our faith into the everyday world. What our ancestors are saying goes something like this:

Because we believe Jesus is the Christ, the only Son of God, we accept him as our Lord, our Master, our Leader. We are his disciples, his faithful followers. Because we believe Jesus is the Christ, the only Son of God, we stand ready to listen and learn from him. We stand ready to do whatever he might ask of us.

If you believe in Jesus as your Lord, then it has to mean the same thing for you. When you believe Jesus is your Lord, too, then you also stand ready to learn from him, ready to do whatever he might ask. Your belief in Jesus will make a difference in how you think and act every day, not just on Sunday. Your belief in and your relationship with Jesus will affect everything you do and say. Your life will center around Jesus, your Lord, just as it did for your ancestors in faith.

You may not have to risk your life to follow Jesus as they did, but you may sometimes have to risk your popularity. You may sometimes have to risk being called a "nerd" or a "wimp." You may sometimes have to go against what today's society says is cool. So when you say you believe in Jesus as your Lord, too, you're making a pledge to live a certain way, not just to think a certain way.

Scripture Search 📖

Read Matthew 5:3–12. In this well-known passage containing the Beatitudes (or "Be-Attitudes," as some have called them), Jesus describes the kind of life to which a Christian is called. Share your responses to the questions that follow.

1. What does it mean to be "poor in spirit"?

2. When have you felt great sorrow? How were you consoled?

3. Who are the "lowly" in today's global society? What is promised them?

4. In your opinion, what did Jesus mean by the words "hunger and thirst for holiness"?

5. Name three ways a person your age might "show mercy."

6. What reward does Jesus promise those who remain faithful to God the Father?

7. How can you be a "peacemaker" at home? In school? In your community?

8. What kinds of "persecution" might a true follower of Christ experience today?

Catechism Corner

The Beatitudes depict the countenance of Jesus Christ and portray his charity. They express the vocation of the faithful . . . they shed light on the actions and attitudes characteristic of the Christian life. . . . (1717)

Journey Within

Write about a time when you went against what society says is "cool," or when you went along with what society says is "cool," even though you knew you were being unfaithful to God. In either case, how did you feel about your actions?

_____

_____

_____

Breakaway
Christian "Cool"

Form a group with two or three of your classmates. Fill in the chart below.

Topics	What society says is cool	What a Christian says is cool
About alcohol or drugs	_____	_____
About sexuality	_____	_____
About material possessions	_____	_____
About violence	_____	_____
About respect for property	_____	_____
About the value of life	_____	_____

Full circle

Here's something worth noting about how our ancestors worded this part of the Creed. It starts with belief in Jesus, whose love, goodness, courage, wisdom, and friendship they had experienced. It expresses belief that this Jesus is, in fact, the very Christ, the Messiah promised by God in ages past. Then it makes the giant leap into the belief that this Jesus is divine. He is the Christ, the only Son of God. After raising us to this lofty level of faith, our ancestors then bring us back to everyday life by reminding us that our faith calls us to practical action as followers of our Lord, Jesus.

Catechism Corner

Very often in the Gospels people address Jesus as "Lord." This title testifies to the respect and trust of those who approach him for help and healing. . . . (Cf. *Mt* 8:2; 14:30; 15:22; *et al.*)

The point is this: your faith—the faith that can guide you throughout the journey of life—embraces all of reality. Many people your age (and many adults, too) tend to think of faith as something that is basically other-worldly. Not so! The faith you express when you pray the Creed is not one-dimensional. It plants one of your feet firmly in the realm of the divine. That's for sure. But it plants your other foot firmly on this earth, to be lived out in your family, in your neighborhood, in your school, in your parish, and in the world.

Breakaway
A Firmly Planted Foot

Using your own foot as a pattern, draw a footprint on a piece of construction paper or tag board. Cut it out and set it aside.

Think about how you—as a follower of Jesus—would deal with each of the following situations. Then select one of the scenarios and write a paragraph describing how you would translate your faith into action. Write your paragraph on your footprint.

With your classmates, make a wall display of footprints.

Situation #1: Several adults with mental disabilities move into a group home in your neighborhood. Some of the residents in the area are opposed to the newcomers living so close to "regular" people. What could you do to show your faith in action?

Situation #2: Your sister used something that belongs to you and damaged it. You got very angry and swore that you would never forgive her. Then you remember the pledge you make to Jesus when you pray the Apostles' Creed. What will you do to be faithful to your pledge?

Situation #3: Every morning, the kids on your bus make fun of the bus driver, who has a hard time trying to keep order. How can you show that you are a follower of Jesus?

Situation #4: Martin has difficulty making friends. At school, no one wants to sit near him or work with him in a small group. During break time, everyone avoids him. How can you show that you believe in the teachings of Jesus?

Situation #5: You and your friend are at the mall. It would be easy to shoplift a CD by your favorite group, your friend insists. Everybody does it, and no one really gets hurt. "C'mon, do it!" your friend urges. How would you show that you are a disciple of Jesus?

Situation #6: Your best friend didn't study for the big science test. You did—and you feel confident that you will do well. Before class, your friend asks you to let her copy from your test paper. "If you're my friend," she says, "you'll help me out." What will you do to show you are a follower of Jesus?

Situation #7: You're playing catch with a friend in your backyard. You throw the ball a little too hard, and it crashes through your neighbor's garage window. Your neighbor's not home—he'll never know how the window got broken, you tell yourself. How could you put your faith into action?

Situation #8: You're standing in line at the snack counter in a movie theater. The woman in front of you pulls some money out of her wallet to pay for popcorn and soda. You see a dollar bill fall to the floor. The woman doesn't know what happened; she doesn't see the money lying next to her shoe. What can you do to show that you want to follow the teachings of the Son of God?

Situation #9: Chandra is a girl in your class. Her mother died recently, after a long illness. When Chandra came back to school, no one in your class knew what to say to her. So no one said anything; they just left her alone. Chandra always looks so sad. How can you show that you are a disciple of Jesus?

Situation #10: You and a group of kids are standing at your locker before morning classes begin. Chad, who says he hates black people, starts telling a joke that puts down blacks. Some of the kids listen to Chad and laugh at the joke. What could you do to show that you have accepted Jesus as your Lord?

Form a small group with several of your classmates. Using chart paper and watercolor markers, make a sketch of a ship (a simple sailboat will do) sailing on the water. Then follow each set of directions below.

1. Brainstorm ten characteristics of a good citizen. Record these in the water.

2. Designate a date for "Good Citizen Day" in your neighborhood or community and give several suggestions for how it should be celebrated. Record your group's ideas in the boat.

3. Nominate several people from your school, neighborhood, or community for a Good Citizenship Award. List their names on the sail.

Present your group's work to the class.

Disciples of Jesus

When you are a good citizen of a country, you believe in its constitution and its way of government. You believe in your flag and what your flag stands for. You believe in your country's ideals of freedom and justice. It's common for a good citizen to say, "I love my country." That's good. But what you actually believe in and love are certain abstract truths, ideals, and values. There's something impersonal and one-sided about being a good citizen. You can't sit down and talk to your flag or your constitution. Your flag and your constitution can't believe in you and love you back.

But when you are a Christian, it's not like that. You believe in and love a very real person—Jesus. Just as important, Jesus believes in you, too, and loves you back! You can talk to Jesus. You can experience Jesus present to you in the Eucharist and the other sacraments. You can become totally united to Jesus in Holy Communion. So being a Catholic Christian is both personal and communal.

POST-IT QUOTE

I am the living bread that came down from heaven. Whoever eats of this bread will live forever. . . . Those who eat my flesh and drink my blood abide in me, and I in them.

John 6:51, 56

That's why your faith makes you a disciple of Jesus. Unlike being a patriot, being a disciple is a person-to-Person relationship. You don't simply believe certain abstract truths about Jesus. You are caught up in a very personal friendship with Jesus. You believe in and seek out Jesus, not some abstract ideals. And Jesus is just as active in seeking you out, calling and guiding and caring for you in very concrete, practical ways.

What's Your View?

Get together with a partner. Share your ideas about how being a disciple is different from being a patriot.

That you believe your friend Jesus is the Christ, the Son of God, doesn't make your friendship less personal. You don't suddenly draw back, saying you aren't good enough or that Christ, the Son of God, is off in some distant heaven and couldn't be interested in you. Rather, you value your friendship with Jesus all the more. You become more eager than ever to be a good, loyal friend to Jesus, helping carry out his mission here on earth. Because you believe your friend Jesus is the Son of God, you feel more confident and safe in your journey through life. You are more eager to tell others about Jesus and more willing to put up with the problems and risks that come with being a friend of Jesus in today's society.

A five-year-old child asks you, "Who is Jesus?" How would you respond?

_____

_____

_____

So when you stand up and publicly say the words "I believe in Jesus Christ, God's only Son, our Lord," you are telling the world that you are a disciple of Jesus, and you are proud of it.

Breakaway

Disciple Saturday

Form a group with several of your classmates. Your group is a parish committee that is responsible for arranging the activities for "Disciple Saturday," a special day in your parish. Plan the liturgy for this day, including appropriate readings and music, and arrange several fun activities to mark this important celebration. Present your plans to the class.

Christian faith and Christian culture

There was a time when just about all the peoples and countries in what we now call Europe were Christian. At that time, the practice of the Christian religion and the everyday life of society were just about identical. For example, most towns had a patron saint. That saint's feast day was a holy day (holiday) for the entire town. Everybody took off from work, went to church, and then had a big party. All the major Christian feasts—such as Christmas, Easter, and All Saints' Day—were celebrated like that all throughout Europe. The calendar we now use has been shaped by the Christian faith. Society began to figure all dates in relation to the year they thought Jesus was born. That's where the older calendar terms _B.C._ (before Christ) and _A.D._ (_Anno Domini_ is Latin for "in the year of our Lord") come from.

We still have many holidays and holiday customs in our country that have their origins in the Christian religion, such as Halloween, Valentine's Day, Mardi Gras, and Saint Patrick's Day. The two biggest holidays of the year—Christmas and Easter—obviously have their roots in our Christian religion.

But the religious meaning in most of these customs is now lost. For example, Halloween, the eve of the Feast of All Saints ("hallowed" means "holy"), used to be considered a holy evening. But now it hardly has a holy meaning. Now it is a time for ghosts and goblins, witches and devils, tricks and vandalism. For many people, Easter—the most important Christian feast of the year—now means spring break, a time to go to some warm climate for a vacation from school or work. It has nothing to do with faith or religion. Similarly, Advent and the Christmas Season seems to be a time when many people focus more on shopping, partying, and Santa Claus than on Jesus and the incarnation. People with no religion of any kind (even atheists who don't believe in the existence of God) celebrate these holidays in our country. So, the fact that we've been influenced by Christian customs doesn't make us a Christian country.

Catechism Corner

. . . Only when Christ is formed in us will the mystery of Christmas be fulfilled in us. . . . (Cf. *Gal* 4:19.) (526)

There are many people, too, who follow Christian principles. They accept and try to follow some of the basic teachings of Jesus: loving their neighbor, showing concern for the poor, condemning violence. This is very good, of course. But this doesn't make them Christians.

To be a true Christian, you need to have a personal friendship with Jesus and you need to believe Jesus is the Son of God and Savior of the world (the Christ). You need to try to live the way Jesus taught in everything you do.

What's Your View?

Get together with a partner. Share your ideas about the difference between being Christian and living in a Christian culture.

So being Christian is more than practicing certain Christian customs. It is more than living by certain Christian principles. Christian customs and principles can give a country a Christian culture. But it takes personal friendship and faith in Jesus to make the people in the country Christians.

 Breakaway
Signs of the Season

Five holidays that have their roots in the Christian faith are given below. In the column labeled **Christian culture**, list several customs often associated with the day. In the column labeled **Christian faith**, tell how the day can be celebrated in true Christian faith.

Holidays	Christian culture	Christian faith
Valentine's Day		
Saint Patrick's Day		
Easter		
Halloween		
Christmas		

Over the centuries since our Creed was first written, our ancestors in faith have continued to think about and dig deeper into those words. They have studied history to learn more about the times in which Jesus lived so they could better understand what the Gospels tell us about his life. They have dug through the whole of the Old Testament to be better able to understand Jesus' role and mission as Christ, the Messiah. They have prayed and pondered over the mystery that Jesus is both truly human and truly God.

In each generation, they have asked themselves what is expected of them as his disciples in their own time in history.

You are starting out with the same unchanging belief in Jesus our ancestors had two thousand years ago. You, too, must dig into the meaning of that belief and ask what is expected of you at this point in history. So being able to say the words of the Creed with real faith isn't the end of your faith journey. It is intended to be the starting point of lifelong growth as a disciple of Jesus.

Reflection

Reader 1: Jesus asked his disciples this question: "Who do people say that the Son of Man is?"

Reader 2: They replied, "Some say John the Baptizer, others Elijah, still others Jeremiah or one of the prophets."

Reader 1: "And you," he said to them, "who do you say that I am?"

Reader 2: "You are the Messiah," Simon Peter answered, "the Son of the living God!"

Reader 1: Jesus replied, "Blest are you, Simon son of Jonah! No man has revealed this to you, but my heavenly Father."

Who do you think Jesus is?

Prayer for Today

God our Father, you have called each of us by name to be one with you.

We thank you for sending us Jesus, your Son, to be our Messiah, model, and friend.

We promise that we will try to live as he did: to be the Christ that others can see.

We ask you to draw us ever closer to you through him. Amen.

HOMEWORK

Design a poster proclaiming your friendship with Jesus and your acceptance of him as your Lord.

Chapter 3

THE WORD MADE FLESH

. . . He was conceived by the power of the Holy Spirit and born of the Virgin Mary.

Setting the Stage: Family Tree

Draw your family tree. Include your immediate family members as well as your grandparents, aunts, uncles, and cousins. If you live in a blended family, your tree will have even more branches!

A word of introduction

Our Creed tells us that Jesus is the Christ, our Lord, and the only Son of God. It is no accident that our ancestors felt it was necessary to complete that description of our belief in Jesus by adding to the Creed the words "who was conceived by the Holy Spirit, born of the Virgin Mary." In this chapter, let's take a closer look at what it is our ancestors were telling us about Jesus when they added those words to our Creed.

To be honest, this chapter is going to be kind of tough. We're at the heart of our faith here. We'll be dealing with what we described in the last chapter as "the mystery of the incarnation." In a sense, we're at the very center of God's plan for all creation and for every human being, including you!

Catechism Corner

Belief in the true Incarnation of the Son of God is the distinctive sign of Christian faith. . . . (463)

The family tree

Though it involves a great mystery, at the time appointed by God, God's only Son became a part of our human family tree. Jesus became our brother. In our Creed, the words "conceived by the Holy Spirit, born of the Virgin Mary" explains how this came about. Unlike the rest of us, Jesus had no human father who participated in his conception. Rather, it was through the power of the Holy Spirit that Jesus was conceived and began to grow within Mary. Because Jesus was conceived through the power of God's Spirit, Jesus retained the divine nature in all its fullness. At the same time, Jesus also assumed from Mary his mother a human nature, like ours in all ways (except sin, of course). He was truly the Son of God while at the same time fully human.

ON YOUR OWN

Read the story of the Annunciation (Luke 1:26–38). Pretend you are Mary writing an entry in your diary describing the events that have just taken place. What would you write? What are you feeling? How will you tell your parents? Who will be the first person you share this amazing event with?

Catechism Corner

. . . Only in the Paschal mystery can the believer give the title "Son of God" its full meaning. (444)

Son of God

In the Old Testament, the messiah is called the *son of God* several times. To the people of that time, this was a title given to angels, the chosen people, and their kings. The title indicated a relationship of particular closeness between God and his creatures. While Jesus lived on earth, those who called him "the son of God" recognized his closeness to God but did not fully recognize the unique and eternal relationship of Jesus to God his Father. Only through Jesus' death and resurrection does the title "Son of God" gain its full meaning.

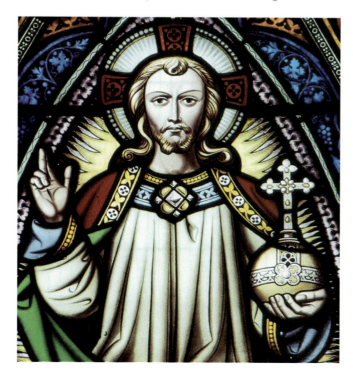

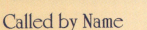

Called by Name

Make a list of the people in the New Testament who referred to Jesus as "Son of God" by researching the following verses.

Scripture references	Name of person speaking
Matthew 16:16	_____
Matthew 27:54	_____
Mark 3:11	_____
Luke 1:35	_____
Luke 4:3	_____
John 1:34	_____
John 1:49	_____
John 5:25	_____
John 20:30	_____

One person

So in a sense, Jesus is like you. He was entirely human. Before his death on the cross, he encountered all of the feelings and many of the experiences that most humans feel and experience. Quite unlike you, Jesus has in addition to his human nature, a divine nature. He is the only Son of the Father; he is God himself. Yet, like you, Jesus is one Person, not two persons.

Catechism Corner

The Son of God . . . worked with human hands; he thought with a human mind. He acted with a human will, and with a human heart he loved. . . . (*GS* 22 § 2.) (470)

Journey Within

To be fully human means to experience the deepest of human emotions: joy, sorrow, anger, fear, pain, contentment. Write about a time when you felt a deep emotion.

_____
_____
_____

What's Your View?

Form a group with two or three of your classmates. Share your responses to the following questions.

1. What does it mean to say that Jesus is "fully divine"?

2. Jesus was fully human, with a human nature. To have a human nature implies experiencing certain feelings that are common to all humans. What feelings or emotions do all humans share that Jesus, too, must have experienced?

3. Jesus was a man of his time. He looked like, talked like, dressed like, and behaved like the people among whom he lived. If Jesus were physically among us today, how would he look, talk, dress, and behave?

4. Share your ideas about how Jesus is like you and how he is unlike you.

It's a mystery

A religious mystery always joins two truths that don't seem to fit together. Each truth taken alone is easy enough to accept. But our mind boggles when we put the two together. God is. That's okay. Man is. That's okay, too. But when we say "God became a human" our mind buckles and balks. Because it is through God's Spirit that Mary became pregnant with Jesus, and not through union with a man, it is called a "virginal conception." Mary is a virgin mother, another seemingly contradictory phrase. Only *in faith* can we accept and then enter into a mystery *of faith*.

What's Your View?

With a small group of your classmates, share your ideas in response to the following questions.

1. People of all ages seem to enjoy mystery stories. In your opinion, why is this so?

2. Name several mystery books, movies, TV programs, or computer programs that have (or have had) wide audiences.

3. How are mystery stories solved?

4. Look up the word *mystery* in a dictionary. Most dictionaries will give several meanings for the word. Which meaning relates to *mystery* stories? Which meaning relates to a *faith* mystery? Why might people find a mystery of faith hard to accept?

Mysteries are like that

One of the many names Catholics have for Mary is the Blessed Virgin Mother. We know what virginity is. We know what motherhood is. But when we start talking about a virgin mother, our mind seems to say, "No way!" We'll say much more about Mary in a minute.

POST-IT QUOTE

If the works of God were such as might be easily comprehended by human reason, they could not be called wonderful or unspeakable.

Thomas À Kempis

Our ancestors summarized and declared our faith in the mystery of the incarnation quite simply in the words "conceived by the Holy Spirit, born of the Virgin Mary."

Catechism Corner

. . . the Incarnation . . . does not mean that Jesus Christ is part God and part man, nor does it imply that he is the result of a confused mixture of the divine and the human. He became truly man while remaining truly God. . . . (464)

So we can say it (just as they did) and believe it (just as they did), but we can't hope to fully understand or explain this mystery. Our ancestors didn't, either. You see, you can't understand and define a divine mystery in the same way you can understand and define a triangle or the law of gravity. You *experience* a mystery. You *enter into* it. You continue to explore it all your life. So rather than trying to define or explain it, let it define you and give shape to your life in the same way our ancestors did.

What's Your View?

Get together with a partner. Share your ideas about how a divine mystery is different from a mystery story.

From the earliest days of Christianity, there have been some people who had a hard time accepting this mystery of the incarnation. So they tried to come up with explanations that completely fit human reason and logic. Each time people tried to do this, guess what happened? They ended up denying some aspect of the mystery.

For example, some people came up with the idea that Jesus was fully divine, but only seemed to be human or was only partly human. Others went in the opposite direction and said he was totally human, but not divine. They said it wasn't until after Jesus' death and resurrection that God "adopted" Jesus and gave him divine qualities.

Even today, there are people who call themselves "Christian" but deny Jesus' divinity. They believe Jesus was perhaps the greatest man who ever lived, but they do not believe he is the Son of God.

Journey Within

A friend asks you, "How can Jesus be God?" How would you respond?

_____

_____

Think of the many roles and responsibilities a mother has. Using the model below, write a job description for motherhood.

_____, _____ individual cares for _____. Must be

able to _____, _____, and _____. Should have

a background in _____ and _____, and be willing to

_____. Desirable personality traits include _____ and

_____. Skills in _____, _____, and

_____ are necessary. Typical duties include _____,

_____, and _____. Above all, individual is responsible for

_____.

Mary, the Mother of Jesus

It's natural that we should honor the mother of Jesus. Mothers play a key role in their child's development. So when someone accomplishes a great feat, at least part of the credit and honor often goes to that person's mother.

POST-IT QUOTE

Throughout the ages no nation has ever had a better friend than the mother who taught her children to pray.

It's natural enough, then, to honor Mary simply for her role in Jesus' formation and development throughout his childhood. She obviously did a great job! But the real reasons for the special honor we show to Mary go far beyond this more or less natural reaction. They are rooted in our faith.

Catechism Corner

From the descendants of Eve, God chose the Virgin Mary to be the mother of his Son. . . . (508)

Mary was hand-picked by God to be the mother of his only Son. We can assume that God is a pretty good judge of people. So for him to pick Mary out of all the women who would ever exist means she was special. And above all, she is special because, by God's grace, she is the Mother of the Son of God.

We believe that Mary is the most important and the most ideal mother who ever existed. Think of as many qualities as you would ever want to find in a good mother: generosity and patience, courage and compassion, gentleness and kindness, wisdom and common sense. Mary had all these qualities in abundance!

So why do we honor Mary? We honor Mary because God the Father honored Mary, and so did her son, Jesus.

The first Christian

To sing Mary's praises isn't the same as making her a goddess. She was human, just as you are. She had to live by faith, just as you do. She had to struggle with doubt and fear. She had to grapple with the mystery of who her son really was, just as you do. In some ways, you may even be better off than she was. Mary was poor and had to put up with the common injustices in her time toward people who were poor. She also spent most of her life working long hours doing the most common tasks such as washing clothes, preparing meals, doing dishes, and cleaning house. In short, don't equate Mary with a fairy-tale princess who lived a charmed life and who couldn't understand what "real life" was like. Mary knew what real life was like.

What makes Mary so special isn't that she never had to put up with the trials and challenges of life. If anything, she had more to face than any of us. What makes Mary special is the way she dealt with all the challenges and trials of life. She sought only to do God's will, to live her life as God wanted her to live it. She put her whole life at God's disposal and never turned back.

Journey Within

We honor Mary because she said "Yes" to God's invitation. She made what we call a "leap of faith." Even though she did not fully understand God's plan for her, she was willing to do as he asked. Because she said "Yes," she is loved and honored as the Mother of God.

Write about a time when you said "Yes" to a new experience that helped you on your journey to adulthood.

_____

_____

_____

Catechism Corner

At the announcement that she would give birth to "the Son of the Most High" without knowing man, by the power of the Holy Spirit, Mary responded with the obedience of faith, certain that "with God nothing will be impossible." . . . (494)

Apart from Jesus, her son, Mary is the most unselfish person who ever lived. Apart from Jesus, no one ever followed God's will so perfectly. In short, Mary was the first person to live completely according to the way Jesus teaches all of us to live. In a real sense, Mary is the first follower of Jesus, the first Christian, the first disciple.

So we honor Mary as a human like us. We honor Mary because, more than anyone else who ever lived, she shows all of us what being a real Christian—a follower of Jesus—is all about. She is a model for the entire Church and the whole human race.

Pray for us

It's not hard to understand why Mary often has been the first one Catholics turn to in prayer. On one hand, she knows the kind of trials and difficulties we face in our daily lives. She faced them, too. On the other hand, no one is closer to God the Father and his Son, Jesus, than Mary. So if anyone can intercede with God for us, it is Mary.

This doesn't mean you can't go directly to Jesus. But it never hurts to go to Jesus with Mary at your side, as it were. In fact, it always pleases Jesus that we honor his mother by praying for her intercession. So it's not surprising that devotion to Mary has been a part of our faith tradition from the beginning

of the Church. Our tradition is filled with special feasts, shrines, prayers, and devotions honoring Mary. In a real sense, part of being Catholic Christian means having a special love for and devotion to Mary, the Mother of the Christ.

Scripture Search

Read about the occasion when Jesus worked his first miracle in John 2:1–11. Then answer the questions that follow.

1. What was being celebrated, and where was the celebration held?

2. What problem did the host experience?

3. Who told Jesus about the host's problem?

4. What advice did this person give the servants?

5. What was the "sign" Jesus performed?

6. This is one of the few times in the Gospels that Mary speaks. What can we learn about her and her relationship to Jesus from this passage?

Several opportunities to honor Mary in a special way are offered in most parishes. Interview your parish priest or representatives of the organizations within your parish that sponsor devotions to Mary. Find out what activities your parish offers in honor of the Blessed Mother. Report your findings to the class.

Virgin Mother

We believe, as our Creed says, that Mary became pregnant and Jesus began to grow within her womb through the power of the Holy Spirit. She became a mother while remaining a virgin. The Catholic Church teaches that, through the power of God, Mary remained a virgin throughout her life. The major point our ancestors focus on by believing in Mary's virginity actually points us to Jesus, not Mary. Our ancestors are expressing their belief in the divine origin and divine nature of Jesus when they express belief in Mary's virginity.

Catechism Corner

. . . Jesus was conceived solely by the power of the Holy Spirit in the womb of the Virgin Mary. . . . (496)

Mary conceived through the power of the Holy Spirit. For her part, Mary was the willing and obedient servant of God who accepted his invitation to be the mother of Jesus. So when we say in the Creed that we believe in Mary's virginity, we aren't expressing the belief that virginity is better than marriage, or that people who marry and become parents are less perfect Christians than those who remain unmarried and virgins. That's not the point of the words "born of the Virgin Mary." Belief in Mary's virginity points us first of all to Jesus' divinity and the Fatherhood of God.

The feasts of Mary

There are two major feasts honoring Mary and the key events in her life. The first feast day is the Solemnity of the Immaculate Conception, celebrated on December 8 each year. On this feast, we celebrate the fact the Mary was conceived free from original sin. The Church teaches that, from the very first moment of her existence, Mary was filled with God's grace and holiness. She was never subject to original sin; she was not born deprived of the gift of God's grace. On this solemnity, then, we celebrate Mary's sinlessness.

The second major feast is the Solemnity of the Assumption of Mary into heaven, celebrated on August 15. It is the belief of the Church that at the end of her life Mary was taken body and soul into heaven.

Because she was the "first Christian," it is only fitting that she be the first to enjoy the fullness of the reward that awaits all of us. We will have to wait until the end of the world for the fullness of the reward, but Mary, the mother of Jesus, has been given this special privilege of bodily assumption.

Using a calendar that marks religious feast days, identify the special feasts of Mary celebrated on these dates:

January 1 _____

May 31 _____

August 22 _____

September 8 _____

September 15 _____

October 7 _____

December 12 _____

In addition, there are various feasts in which Mary plays a key part, even if they aren't devoted directly to her. These include the feast of the Annunciation of the Lord, celebrated on March 25. On this feast, we recall and celebrate the event described in that part of our Creed we talked about in this chapter. God sent an angel to invite Mary to become the mother of Jesus, and she agreed. Because she agreed, the power of the Holy Spirit overshadowed her and she became pregnant with Jesus. The most obvious solemnity is Christmas, the Church's celebration of the birth of Jesus. Others include the Feast of the Holy Family and the Solemnity of the Epiphany, celebrated on the two Sundays that follow Christmas. Then there is the feast of Jesus' Presentation in the Temple on February 2. So throughout the year, the Church continually honors Mary, the mother of Jesus and our mother, too.

Journey Within

We honor our mothers in a special way each Mother's Day. What gift will you give Mary this Mother's Day? Why?

Reflection

A reading from the Gospel of Luke 1:46–55.

> And Mary said,
> "My soul magnifies the Lord,
>   and my spirit rejoices in God my Savior,
> for he has looked with favor on the lowliness of his servant.
> Surely, from now on all generations will call me blessed;
> for the Mighty One has done great things for me,
> and holy is his name.
> His mercy is for those who fear him
> from generation to generation.
> He has shown strength with his arm;
> he has scattered the proud in the thoughts of their hearts.
> He has brought down the powerful from their thrones
> and lifted up the lowly;
> He has filled the hungry with good things,
> and sent the rich away empty.
> He has helped his servant Israel,
> in remembrance of his mercy,
> according to the promise he made to our ancestors,
> to Abraham and to his descendants forever."

What do you personally find most appealing about Mary? Why?

Prayer for Today

God our Father, we echo Mary's glorious prayer of praise to you. Grace us with your Holy Spirit so that we may say "Yes" as she did to your invitation to the fullness of life. Blessed Mary, our heavenly mother, guide us gently along the path of goodness so that we may be united forever with you and your Son, our Lord Jesus Christ. Amen.

Across

4. One who devotes himself or herself to meeting the needs of others

5. This mystery refers to Jesus' having two natures: human and divine.

7. This is one way to speak to God.

8. Belief

9. Mary's relationship to Jesus

10. Persons who do not marry and have children, such as priests and sisters

11. To receive from one's parents through heredity

13. Jesus shares this kind of nature with us.

Down

1. Because he is God, Jesus has this kind of nature.

2. We honor Mary because she was a _____ human.

3. A map of one's ancestors, showing their interrelationships

6. One who believes in and follows the teaching of Jesus

9. A religious truth that cannot be fully explained but can still be believed

12. Great respect, high regard

Chapter 4

THE GOOD NEWS

. . . suffered under Pontius Pilate, was crucified, died, and was buried. He descended to the dead. On the third day he rose again. He ascended into heaven, and is seated at the right hand of the Father. He will come again to judge the living and the dead.

Setting the Stage: The Good News Gazette

Form a group with four or five of your classmates. Share orally one or two items of good news—positive things that have happened to you in the past few days. Using materials supplied by your teacher, create *The Good News Gazette*. (A *gazette* is a newspaper or journal.) Write brief accounts of the group's "good news" in newspaper article format. Post *The Good News Gazette* in a prominent place in your classroom.

The gospel in a nutshell

Up to now, the Creed has focused on who our God is and who our Lord Jesus is. Now the Creed shifts gears. It turns to what Jesus has done for us. In the few lines of the Creed quoted at the beginning of this chapter, our ancestors give us a complete summary of the gospel, the good news about the salvation of our world. The word *gospel* itself means "good news."

The four Gospels we have today didn't appear in written form right away. The written versions of the Gospels we read and listen to today took shape gradually, over a period of some seventy years or more. The gospel story itself was first handed down by word of mouth. The "oral gospel" from which the four written Gospels developed was very simple. Its central message was the story of Jesus' passion, his death, and his resurrection. We call these events the Paschal mystery.

 Breakaway

Get the Message?

If you read the Gospels according to Matthew, Mark, Luke, and John, you will notice several differences among them, even though they tell basically the same story. These differences are due, in part, to the purpose, style, and point of view of the writers. They are also due to the fact that accounts handed down by word of mouth are often altered in each retelling.

To see whether this is true even today, conduct this simple "test" in your classroom. Have five or six students leave the room. As a class, select one newspaper or magazine article (about three or four paragraphs in length) and familiarize yourselves with its content.

Invite one of the students back into the classroom. Tell this student what the newspaper article is all about, filling in all the important details.

Then invite another one of the students back into the classroom. Have the first student retell the story he or she heard from you to the new student. Listen closely. How well did the first student recount what you told him or her? Continue the process, having the second student retell the story to the third, the third to the fourth, and so on until all the students who left the room have retold the story.

• How close was the final retelling to the original story?

• Was the central message of the article retained throughout all retellings?

• In your opinion, how well did the authors of the Gospels do in telling the good news?

The Paschal mystery, the most central part of the gospel message, is what the Creed calls us to believe: that Jesus suffered and died for us sinners, but then God raised Jesus from death, thus freeing us from the destructive power of sin and death forever. Because of Jesus, we no longer have to be enslaved by the power of sin and everlasting death.

That's the "good news" we believe as Christians. You've heard all the words before. But in this chapter, we're going to try to help you form a more mature idea of what faith in this good news really means for you and for the whole world.

Breakaway

What's News?

Get together with a partner. Use the clues below to help you fill in the puzzle blanks. (Hint: Your text can give you lots of help!) When you have the numbered items completed, the letters in the squares will spell out the answer to this question: What important message do the Gospels give us?

1. This word means "good news."
2. The Supreme Being, our Father in heaven
3. Jesus suffered and _____ for us.
4. By his death and _____, Jesus has redeemed us.
5. Before the Gospels were _____, they were told by word of mouth.
6. The Son of God, he is "the Christ"
7. Experienced physical and mental anguish
8. Words sent from one person or group to another
9. Spoken
10. To accept as true or real
11. Jesus' suffering that preceded his death
12. This is a violation of God's law of love.

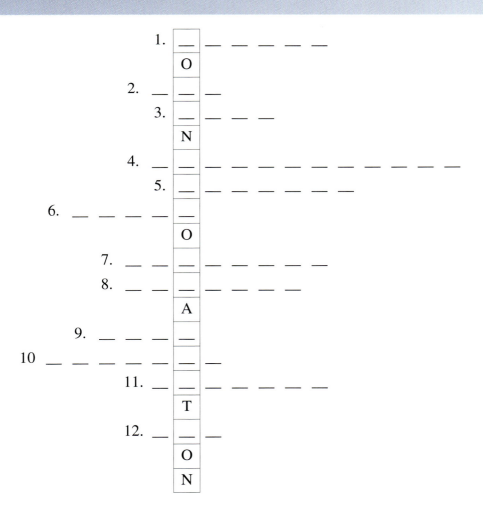

Humpty Dumpty humanity

In a sense, Humpty Dumpty summarizes the history of humanity, but our history isn't a Mother Goose rhyme. As a race, we humans have fallen also. Like Humpty Dumpty, we couldn't put ourselves back together again. Our very first ancestors decided to break from God and try to make it entirely on their own. As a result, they fell flat on their faces, and that's where humanity stayed—helpless, unable to get up, unable to restore the original peace, happiness, unity, and order they lost by turning away from God.

Scripture Search

Read Genesis, chapter 3, to renew your acquaintance with the story of the first humans. This story is designed to teach or explain a truth about humankind.

• What is the truth this story teaches?

Using tiny pieces of colored construction paper, create a mosaic that illustrates in symbols our separation from God as recounted in the story of the first humans. Glue your mosaic to a large sheet of construction paper.

It takes no genius to see that our fallen world today continues to suffer the effects of original sin. It is still filled with problems, despite all our knowledge, our wealth, and our science. Poverty, starvation, crime, violence, injustice, hatred, jealousy, greed, loneliness, and illness are everywhere. If you look out at the world that you are going to live in as an adult, it can seem pretty grim and hopeless. It would be easy enough for you to say, "We can't ever be put together again."

 Breakaway

A Fallen World

Form a group with two or three of your classmates. Search through newspapers and magazines for headlines and articles that show the world still suffers the effects of original sin. Mount your findings on a piece of poster board. Give your work a title.

Our ancestors in faith had no trouble seeing the world as a fallen world, enslaved by the power of sin and condemned to suffer all the effects of its sins, the ultimate effect being death itself. Because they could see the "bad news" all around them, they longed for redemption, for some "good news." That is also why they were able to see and believe in the "good news" of redemption when it came in the form of the life, death, and resurrection of Jesus.

Get together with a partner. Search through newspapers and magazines for headlines and articles that show the world is affected by the "good news" and redeeming grace of the Paschal mystery. Mount your findings on a piece of poster board. Give your work a title.

Journey Within

For many people, the world seems a grim and hopeless place. What fears about the world—and your future—do you have? Tell God about them. Adolescents are often noted for being idealistic thinkers. What are your hopes for the world you will work and live in as an adult? Tell God about them.

_____

_____

_____

Redemption: How God brought it about

Think of the last time you were really sick, maybe with the flu. You were flat on your back, weak and helpless, feeling so terrible you couldn't even watch television or listen to your favorite CDs. You couldn't keep anything in your stomach. Then someone—a parent, sibling, or other caregiver—"redeemed" you. How? Though healthy, he or she took on the effects of your sickness. That person became one with you in your sickness. You were confined to bed. That person changed his or her schedule, maybe stayed home from work, to be with you. In short, he or she became "confined" with you. You were weak and tired. Your caregiver became tired, too, losing sleep to care for you. You couldn't eat. Your caregiver had his or her own meals disrupted in order to care for you. So your caregiver entered into your sickness and then used his or her own health and strength to help you become well and strong again.

That's how redemption works. The one doing the redeeming gets right down on the ground with the fallen person. The redeemer enters into the pain and weakness of the fallen person. The redeemer becomes united with the fallen person in order to share his or her strength and raise the fallen person. That's what Jesus did.

Journey Within

Write about a time when you were a "redeemer" to a friend or family member.

_____

_____

_____

. . . Was crucified, died, and was buried

Two qualities—love for one another and total trust in God—were the qualities often missing in the fallen world. Two attitudes—selfishness and disregard for neighbor and indifference to and lack of trust in God's love—were the source of all the suffering and misery in the fallen world. They ultimately led to the death all people faced.

What's especially bad about this is the fact that everybody became victims of the suffering, ignorance, and death that original sin caused. Good people suffered, too, including innocent babies and children and the elderly. In such a world, a person didn't have to be a sinner to become a victim of the effects of sin.

POST-IT QUOTE ☑

You have an ego—a consciousness of being an individual. But that doesn't mean that you are to worship yourself, to think constantly of yourself, and to live entirely for self.

Billy Graham

This is the world Jesus entered. Through all his life, Jesus primarily did two things. First, he never stopped loving others, even his enemies who put him to death. Second, he never stopped trusting in his Father's love for him, no matter how hopeless things seemed. These two personal qualities—total love for others and total trust in God his Father—are basically what Jesus taught by his words and actions. These are the two qualities that made Jesus healthy and strong (sinless) in a fallen (sinful) world. Through the incarnation the Son of God joined humanity. The reason for the incarnation was to fulfill the Father's plan to redeem humanity. Through Jesus' suffering and death, we have been redeemed.

POST-IT QUOTE

As the Father has loved me, so I have loved you; abide in my love.

John 15:9

What's Your View?

Form a group with three or four of your classmates. Share your responses to the following questions.

1. A song by the music group Hanson is titled, "Where Is the Love?" Do you think there are many people in the world who are asking that question today? Explain your answer.

2. Why do many people find it difficult to express—both in words and actions—love for another?

3. How does Jesus' message of love for our neighbor conflict with what modern society sometimes tells us to feel toward our neighbor? Give examples to support your answer.

4. In your opinion, which is more difficult: to place your trust in other people or to place your trust in God? Explain your answer.

Though Jesus was totally sinless, he united himself completely with sinful people, so much so that he freely accepted the effects of that sinfulness. Though innocent, he was condemned as a dangerous criminal, an enemy of both government and religion. He was tortured. Then he was nailed to a cross and left to die.

Our natural reaction is to hate those who unfairly cause us suffering. We want to get even, to return evil for evil. All the while, we also tend to complain about a God who lets injustice and evil happen. But through all his suffering, Jesus never stopped loving others, even the people who tortured and killed him. He returned good for evil. He never stopped believing that God the Father loved him and would not abandon him. Even as he hung there, dying on the cross, he continued to trust in his Father.

Scripture Search

1. Read Luke 23:33–34. How did Jesus return good for evil?

2. Read Luke 23:46. How did Jesus continue to show trust in his Father, even at the moment of his death?

ON YOUR OWN

Helping to Carry the Cross

During his passion, even when death was near, Jesus showed his unfailing love for others. He asks us to do the same in our daily lives by helping someone who is carrying a cross of grief, loneliness, illness, or disability by offering an act of kindness to them. For example, you might visit an elderly person in a care center, shovel the sidewalk free of charge for a neighbor who is unable to do so, or send a card offering your support and prayers to a person who may be dealing with a health problem or difficult situation.

So Jesus broke out of this cycle of sin our world was trapped in. He didn't return evil for evil. He didn't give up on God his Father. How much Jesus suffered isn't the issue. What is more important is how Jesus reacted to his suffering—not with hate, but with love; how Jesus reacted to the death he experienced—not by giving up on God the Father, but by continuing to trust in his Father's love.

That's what we believe when we say the words ". . . suffered under Pontius Pilate, was crucified, died, and was buried." We believe Jesus united himself completely with our slavery to sin and its effects. But unlike us, he was able to break free from this slavery and thus free us. Through his death, Jesus reconciled us with his Father.

Journey Within

Imagine that you have a friend who has never heard about Jesus. How would you explain to him or her who Jesus is and what he did for us?

_____

_____

_____

On the third day, he rose again

When Jesus died and was buried, it seemed that evil had won. It seemed that sin and death had conquered love and life. But then God the Father raised Jesus from the tomb, transformed and glorious. He had battled sin and death head-on, on their turf, by becoming one with us. And he won! The risen Jesus became living proof that love and life are more powerful than sin and death. Because of Jesus, we are free!

Catechism Corner

. . . By his glorious Cross Christ has won salvation for all men. He redeemed them from the sin that held them in bondage. . . . (1741)

But the world still suffers from evil. Everyone still dies. So you may be wondering, "Where is the victory and the freedom?" It's kind of like this. It's as if we are being held prisoners in a cell in a deep dungeon. We are held by iron bars and chains and watched by strong, cruel guards. Jesus comes in, drives off the guards, and breaks our chains. We're free! But wait a minute. Suppose we choose to just sit there in that cell, deep in that dungeon. We make no effort to get up and walk out of the cell, up the stairs, and out into the open. Though we could be free, we choose to stay imprisoned.

Our redemption is like that. Jesus makes it possible for us to be free from the powers of sin and everlasting death. But we must still *choose* to be free. This calls for both faith and action on our part.

We need to believe that love and life can conquer sin and death, that redemption is ours through Jesus. Then we need to act that way. We need to believe that, with Jesus' power, we, too, can break the cycle of hatred and selfishness. And then we need to try to love others, even when they may not seem to deserve it. We need to believe that, no matter how bad things may get, God will never abandon us. Then we need to try to face life's problems and our own failures with confidence and courage.

So redemption is ours through Jesus. By his resurrection, Jesus brought the promise of resurrection and eternal life with God to all people.

He ascended into heaven . . .

In those words our ancestors are telling us two things. First, the victory of Jesus is now complete. His visible, "in person" work on earth is completed. He has returned to God the Father who sent him to save us. Second, it's our turn now. Jesus now depends on us to continue his work. Through our belief in Jesus and our Baptism, we receive Jesus' own Spirit. We become his representative, his disciple. So now it's our turn to show the world how to love their neighbor and trust in God. It's our turn to show by our actions that love and life can conquer sin and death. It's our turn to announce the good news of redemption to others by *being* "good news."

He will come . . .

God had a wonderful plan for humanity when we were first created. We were to live in peace and love and justice. This plan got sidetracked when the first humans sinned. Through Jesus, God's plan—the reign of God announced by Jesus—is now back on track. And despite how bad things can seem, we believe, as these words of our Creed proclaim, that at the end of time God's plan will be fulfilled. So just as our Hebrew ancestors waited for the messiah, we now live in hope, waiting for Jesus to come again. We await that end time when peace and love and justice will be restored perfectly. We pray every day "Your kingdom come." We believe that Jesus, as Judge, will oversee the coming of God's reign in its fullness.

This doesn't mean that, as followers of Jesus, we are to sit around doing nothing. As we just said, our task as disciples is to work to help God's plan come about. We are to try to overcome evil and hatred and injustice wherever we see it now. We are to try to promote justice now. We are to try to be peacemakers now. But we do all this knowing that we aren't working alone and knowing that we may never see the plan come fully true in our lifetime. We do this in faith and hope, convinced that at the time of our death, we will be judged on our works, our faith, and our love. We do this convinced that Jesus *will* come again at the end of time and that all those who have died with Christ will share in his resurrection.

Breakaway

Your Kingdom Come

With a group of your classmates, brainstorm ideas on how we can help foster the reign of God in our homes, schools, neighborhoods, cities, nations, and the world. Here are several questions to help you focus your thoughts.

1. What goals should we pursue if we are to carry on Christ's mission?
2. How can we be peacemakers?
3. How can we love unselfishly?
4. How can we work against injustice?
5. How can we share and replenish the earth's resources?
6. How can we return good for evil?
7. How can we show respect for others and their property?
8. How can we care for those who are unable to meet their needs?
9. How can we show that we value life?
10. How can we live as Jesus did?

Write your group's ideas on strips of construction paper. Loop each strip through another, making a paper "chain of salvation." Attach the ends of the chain between the posters you made in the **Fallen World** and **Redeemed World** poster activities earlier in this lesson. Suspend the posters in your classroom to visualize the "chain of salvation" changing the fallen world to the redeemed world.

Some facts, some faith

We haven't talked about a few of the other phrases in this portion of the Creed. First, our ancestors made it clear that Jesus suffered "under Pontius Pilate." It may seem like a small thing, but it is actually very important. They wanted to be sure that people understood they were talking about an historical event. The gospel story wasn't a myth. It really happened, at a definite time and in a definite place. At the time our ancestors developed the Creed, Rome still ruled the known world. Pontius Pilate was a Roman prefect who served in Jerusalem at a certain time. By including him in the Creed, they are, in effect, saying, "This really happened."

ON YOUR OWN

Check It Out

Ask the librarian for help in locating information about Pontius Pilate and the area he ruled during the time of Jesus. Report your findings to the class.

Our ancestors didn't know exactly what happens when a person dies. They believed, like us, that because people have immortal souls they continue to exist after death in some way or another. The words "He descended into hell and on the third day he rose again" indicate that after Jesus' death and before his resurrection, Jesus journeyed into this land of the dead. When Jesus entered into that experience, or experienced the effects of death with all those who had died, he opened heaven's gates for the just who had died before him. By saying, "he descended into hell," our ancestors were expressing their belief that Jesus really experienced death just as all the people who had lived before him.

POST-IT QUOTE

The one thing certain about life is that we must leave it.
Author unknown

Catechism Corner

. . . Jesus, like all men, experienced death and in his soul joined the others in the realm of the dead. But he descended there as Savior, proclaiming the Good News to the spirits imprisoned there. (Cf. *1 Pet* 3:18–19.) (632)

Be Ready

Read the obituary column of your local paper. Note the ages of all those who have died. Add the ages together and divide by the number of people who are listed. What is the average age of those who have died?

"The third day" is a reference to the prophecies in Scripture and Jesus' own statements that he would be raised up from death on the third day. Our ancestors were basically saying, "See? It happened just as the Scriptures said it would and as God planned. We aren't making this up."

Catechism Corner

. . . The Resurrection of Jesus is the crowning truth of our faith in Christ . . . (638)

"At the right hand of the Father" refers to a custom and is an imaginative way of saying Jesus is now in the place of highest honor with his Father. At the time the Creed was developed (and today, too), "at the right hand" meant the place of honor. By referring to this custom, our ancestors were saying they believe that, together with God the Father, Jesus deserves the highest praise and adoration we can give.

50

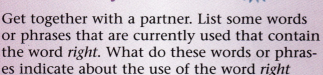
Get together with a partner. List some words or phrases that are currently used that contain the word *right*. What do these words or phrases indicate about the use of the word *right* today?

Finally, to judge "the living and the dead" expresses our ancestors' belief that, as it says in the Gospels, Jesus will appear at the end of time. It could happen tomorrow. It may not happen for the next 10,000 years. No matter. Since we don't know, we, "the living," need always to be ready.

POST-IT QUOTE ☑

For the Lord himself, with a cry of command, wth the archangel's call and with the sound of God's trumpet, will descend from heaven, and the dead in Christ will rise first.

Thessalonians 4:16

Children, it is the last hour!

1 John 2:18

Scripture Search

Read the passages indicated and then answer the questions.

1. Matthew 25:31–46: How does Jesus say he will judge people at the end of time?
2. Luke 12:35–40: To what does Jesus compare his second coming?
3. Mark 13:5–31: How should we apply the lesson of the fig tree to our waiting for the second coming of Jesus?

Journey Within

What are you doing to prepare yourself for Jesus' return?

_____

_____

_____

_____

Reflection

A reading from St. Paul's First Letter to the Corinthians 15:20–22.

But in fact Christ has been raised from the dead, the first fruits of those who have died. For since death came through a human being, the resurrection of the dead has also come through a human being; for as all die in Adam, so all will be made alive in Christ.

What fears about death and dying do you have?

What promise did Jesus make to us about the new life that awaits beyond our death?

Prayer for Today

Side One: *Jesus, our brother, you are God the Father's greatest gift to us.*

Side Two: *By becoming one with us, you have redeemed us.*

Side One: *Help us remember that we are a chosen people, destined for eternal life with you and the Father.*

Side Two: *Help us be the good news of salvation to those we touch in our words and actions.*

Side One: *Strengthen our resolve to lift our world beyond the grasp of loneliness, poverty, greed, and injustice.*

Side Two: *Be with us always as we prepare for your glorious second coming.*

All: *Maranatha. Amen.*

HOMEWORK

Create a "Good News" calendar. Select one day from each month for the next twelve months. On that day, be "good news" for someone special to you—a family member, friend, classmate, or teacher, for example. Do some planning in the chart below.

Month and day	Person	How I will be "good news"
January		
February		
March		
April		
May		
June		
July		
August		
September		
October		
November		
December		

Chapter 5

THE HOLY SPIRIT

I (We) believe in the Holy Spirit (the Lord, the giver of life, who proceeds from the Father and the Son. With the Father and the Son, he is worshiped and glorified. He has spoken through the prophets.)

Setting the Stage: Signs of the Spirit

In the Holy Scriptures, the Holy Spirit is symbolized in several ways. With a partner or a small group of your classmates, make a list of these symbols. Then create a collage of these symbols. (To help you develop your list, read these passages: Genesis 1:1–3; Exodus 13:21–22; Luke 9:34–35; Matthew 3:16; Acts 2:2–3.)

Introduction

For this chapter on the Holy Spirit, we added some words about the Spirit not found in the Apostles' Creed. They come from the Nicene Creed, which the Church developed after the Apostles' Creed was developed. The words we borrowed from the later Creed help us understand better what it is we believe about the Holy Spirit. These words show how our faith deepened and grew—and continues to deepen and grow. These words from the Nicene Creed are like the details a mapmaker might add to the original map of Lewis and Clark that we talked about earlier in the course.

These borrowed words give us an outline of just what it is we do believe when we say the simple words, "I (We) believe in the Holy Spirit." That's what we'll be exploring in this chapter.

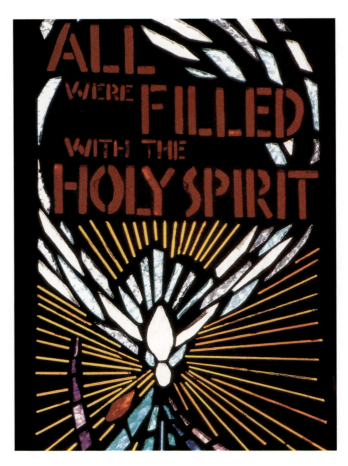

Catechism Corner

. . . to be in touch with Christ, we must first have been touched by the Holy Spirit. . . . (683)

Breakaway
The Power of "One"

The prefix *mono-* means "one." With a partner, determine the words that belong in each of the following statements. Each word will begin with the prefix *mono-*.

1. A _____ is a large block of stone used in architecture or sculpture.

2. A _____ is exclusive control of a business or resource. (It is also the name of a popular board game!)

3. A _____ is a long speech by one person. (Comedians like Jay Leno and David Letterman often begin their act with this.)

4. A _____ is a design composed of one or more initials of a name.

5. _____ is knowing or using only one language.

6. _____ is marriage to one person at a time.

7. A _____ is an airborne vehicle with only one pair of wings.

8. A _____ is an eyeglass for one eye.

9. Something that is _____ has only one color.

10. A _____ is a succession of sounds or words uttered in a single tone of voice.

More than a figure of speech

Unlike most other peoples and nations of their time, the Hebrew people were strict *monotheists*. That is, they believed there was only one almighty God, who created and controls the entire universe. But as they described their relationship with God in the Scriptures over the centuries, they often talked of the action of God's word or God's wisdom. They also often talked of the power and action of the spirit of God, sent upon some prophet or upon the people as a whole.

These could seem to be figures of speech, like saying "The principal's word is law," or "When the teacher arrived, her cheerful spirit filled the whole room." But as you read the Old Testament, you will find many passages that give you the sense that God's word (*logos*, wisdom) and God's spirit have a "personality" all their own. For example, God's wisdom is described like this in the Book of Proverbs:

> . . . then I [God's wisdom] was beside him [God], like a master worker; and I was daily his delight, rejoicing before him always, rejoicing in his inhabited world and delighting in the human race. (Proverbs 8:30–31)

So when the apostles and the early Church pondered Jesus, all he said and did, and all the events surrounding his life, death, and resurrection, they came to realize this word (or wisdom, or *logos*) talked about in the Scriptures was none other than Jesus, the Word made flesh.

In the same way, they came to realize that the Advocate or Spirit whom Jesus promised to send upon them was more than a figure of speech. It was none other than God's Spirit spoken of so often in the Old Testament. God's Spirit was also a divine Person, as are God the Father and Jesus, the Word.

Scripture Search

Read the passages listed to discover the various names for the Holy Spirit used by Paul. Fill in the blanks with the appropriate letters of each word. Then transfer the numbered letters to the last set of blanks to discover the name for the Holy Spirit used by Jesus in John 14:16.

Galatians 3:14   the __ __ __ __ __ __ __ of the Spirit
                             1   6

Romans 8:15   the Spirit of __ __ __ __ __ __ __ __
                                       2

2 Corinthians 3:17   the Spirit of the __ __ __ __
                                          5   3

Romans 8:9   the Spirit of __ __ __ __ __ __
                                      4   7

Romans 8:14   the Spirit of __ __ __

What word did Jesus use for the Holy Spirit? __ __ __ __ __ __ __ __ __
                                             1 2 3 2 4 5 6 7 6

Thus the words "I believe in the Holy Spirit" express this unique Christian belief that the Holy Spirit described in the Old Testament is a divine Person, equal to but distinct from the Father and the Son.

What's Your View?

Get together with a partner and share your ideas about what beliefs we as Catholic Christians hold about the Holy Spirit.

If the Holy Spirit is a Divine Person . . .

. . . then our God is a Trinitarian God! And that is exactly what is at the foundation of our Creed. A basic belief of our Catholic Christian faith is our belief in the Trinity. Like the children of Abraham, we believe there is only one God, but unlike the Jews (or the believers of any other faith, for that matter), we also believe that this one God is three divine Persons! The Father, Son, and Spirit are three distinct Persons, each sharing equally in all the qualities of one divine nature. Each is infinitely powerful, infinitely wise, infinitely everything. That's why we say in the Creed that like the Father and the Son, the Holy Spirit "is worshiped and glorified."

Journey Within

Think of the many gifts and talents God has given you. How might you share these gifts and talents with others?

_____

_____

Catechism Corner

The One whom the Father has sent into our hearts, the Spirit of his Son, is truly God. (Cf. *Gal* 4:6.) . . . (689)

It is through Jesus that we come to know about the Holy Trinity. There is no complete, logical explanation for how the Father, Son, and Spirit can each be God and yet there is only one God. We are at the heart of divine mystery—and faith—when we express our belief in the Trinity. There are comparisons that help a little, like the famous one made by Saint Patrick, who taught his new converts that the Trinity is like a shamrock. Just as three shamrock petals share the common life of the stem, the three divine Persons share one divine nature. But no comparison in nature is quite like the real thing.

This much is certain: Our God is a community of three divine Persons who share completely with each other all that they have and are. Jesus' command that we love one another and share all that we have with each other is an invitation for us humans to imitate the very inner life of God. At the core of the life of our Trinitarian God is a life of total, mutual love and total, mutual sharing. God is love!

The Lord and Giver of Life

If the inner life of God is a life of love, then the Holy Spirit is this divine life of love personified. We are created to participate in God's life. We are given the ability to do this because the Father and Son share with us their own love, their own Spirit. The Father and Son send forth their Holy Spirit on all creation so that we can experience and participate in this divine life of love. That's why we say in our Creed that we believe that the Holy Spirit is the Lord and Giver of this divine life of love. Another name for this divine life of love is *grace*.

POST-IT QUOTE

God's love has been poured into our hearts through the Holy Spirit who has been given to us.
Romans 5:5

Catechism Corner

Grace is first and foremost the gift of the Spirit who justifies and sanctifies us. . . . (2003)

That's why, at the core of all authentic human love, at the core of all true spiritual life is the power and action of the Holy Spirit, sent forth from the Father and the Son. In one of his letters, Paul describes what authentic love (and the action of the Holy Spirit) is like. Paul writes:

Love is patient; love is kind; love is not envious or boastful or arrogant or rude. It does not insist on its own way; it is not irritable or resentful; it does not rejoice in wrongdoing, but rejoices in the truth. It bears all things, believes all things, hopes all things, endures all things.

Love never ends. But as for prophecies, they will come to an end; as for tongues, they will cease; as for knowledge, it will come to an end. (1 Corinthians 13:4–8)

Breakaway
The Real Thing

Society's ideas about love can differ greatly from what Paul says about authentic love. One big difference is that "false" love—the kind of misguided "love" that society seems to teach—is self-serving, while authentic love is other-serving. With a partner or a small group of your classmates, record your ideas about "false" love and authentic love. Then share your ideas with the rest of the class.

False love says if you love me, you will . . .

_____

_____

_____

_____

Authentic love says because I love you, I will . . .

_____

_____

_____

_____

Journey Within

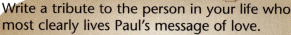

Write a tribute to the person in your life who most clearly lives Paul's message of love.

_____

_____

_____

In another letter, Paul again describes the kind of life the Holy Spirit gives us. In this passage, he refers to what the Catholic Church refers to as the "fruits of the Holy Spirit."

. . . the fruit of the Spirit is love, joy, peace, patience, kindness, generosity, faithfulness, gentleness, and self-control. . . . If we live by the Spirit, let us also be guided by the Spirit. (Galatians 5:22–23, 25)

That should give you a fairly good idea of what happens when you come under the influence of the Holy Spirit. It should also give you a glimpse into what the inner, community life of the Trinity is like.

ON YOUR OWN

The Fruits of the Spirit

Draw a symbol for each fruit of the Holy Spirit given below. Which fruit is most abundant in your life? In what ways can you see the fruits of the Spirit at work in you?

Love	Joy	Peace
Patience	Kindness	Goodness
Truthfulness	Gentleness	Self-control

Journey Within

Paul says that the more we renounce ourselves (that is, the more we become selfless), the more we "work by the Spirit." Write about one aspect of your life where you might make an effort to renounce yourself. How can you be less self-centered and more other-centered?

_____

_____

_____

_____

_____

Who spoke through the prophets

It's rather easy to visualize Jesus, the second Person of the Trinity. And the image of Father helps us imagine what the first Person of the Trinity is like. But how do you imagine a spirit? That's why we use a variety of images to describe the Holy Spirit and the way the Holy Spirit influences us, helping us grow in a life of love for each other. You discovered and worked with some of these images in the introductory activity for this chapter.

The Holy Spirit comes like a gentle dove. The Holy Spirit comes like the whisper of a summer breeze among the leaves. The Holy Spirit comes like a small flame that enlightens and warms. The Holy Spirit heals, beautifies, and strengthens us like warm, perfumed oil flowing over our body. But the Holy Spirit can also come like a raging hurricane that nothing can resist. The Holy Spirit can come like a roaring flame that sets everything on fire.

Catechism Corner

Through the prophets, God forms his people in the hope of salvation . . . (64)

Breakaway
Touched by the Spirit

Form a small group with several of your classmates. Explain the ideas, images, and feelings that you associate with each of the following. In your opinion, why did the writers of the Scriptures use these elements of creation to symbolize the Holy Spirit?

Symbol	My ideas, images, and feelings	Scripture writer's ideas and images
Dove		
Light		
Breeze		
Small flame		
Warm, perfumed oil		
Strong wind		
Roaring fire		

We find the action of the Holy Spirit described in all these ways in the Scriptures. The Holy Spirit comes to comfort and bring peace, to seal with holiness, to heal and restore to life, to enlighten, to strengthen, to empower and move people to action in God's name. The Holy Spirit sets people on fire with love for God, and the Holy Spirit speaks through the prophets.

Journey Within

The Holy Spirit enlivens and empowers you. Write about a time when you met a challenge successfully. Did you feel the Spirit at work in you?

_____

_____

_____

Who's Who?

The abbreviations of several of the prophetic books of the Hebrew Scriptures are used as clues for this crossword puzzle. Use your Bible to discover the full name of each book and the prophet for whom it is named. Complete the puzzle.

Across
2. Jon
5. Ez
8. Hos
9. Mal
11. Is
14. Ob
15. Hag

Down
1. Jer
3. Hab
4. Zech
6. Zeph
7. Jl
9. Mic
10. Dan
12. Am
13. Nah

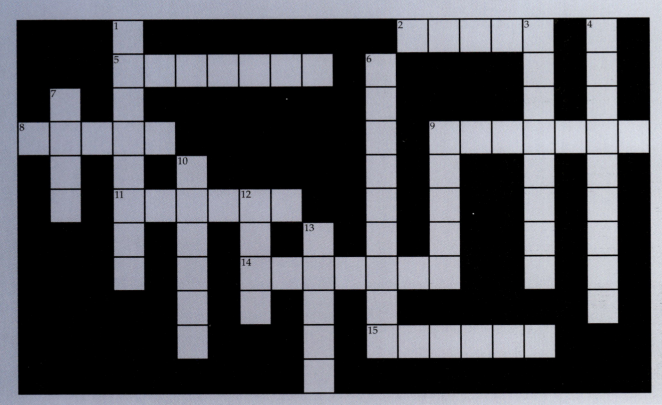

In the time before Jesus, prophets were people who were inspired (inspirited, filled with the Holy Spirit) and who spoke out in the name of God. Because they were filled with the Holy Spirit, prophets were gifted with a highly-developed spiritual sensitivity, a kind of finely-tuned "spiritual radar." This enabled them to recognize even the slightest action or movement of God among the people. It also enabled them to recognize the presence of evil forces at work, even when others didn't. They could also see the long-range consequences if the people continued to cooperate with those evil forces.

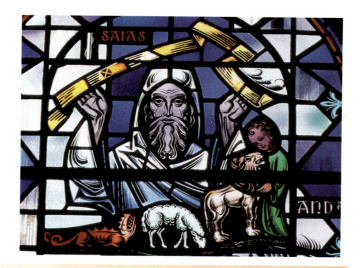

Scripture Search

The prophet Jeremiah was a compelling figure who was often rejected by his own people. Jeremiah made impassioned pleas to the people to be faithful to their covenant with God. He predicted the fall of Jerusalem and the destruction of the Temple, which was the center of religious culture and worship among the Hebrews.

Read Jeremiah 1:4–10 to learn about Jeremiah's call to prophecy. Then answer the questions as Jeremiah might have if he were being interviewed by a modern-day celebrity such as Oprah Winfrey, Rosie O'Donnell, or David Letterman.

Q. When did you receive God's "call" to be a prophet?

A. _____

Q. What was your first reaction to this "call"?

A. _____

Q. How do you know what to tell people?

A. _____

Q. What do you believe God wants you to do?

A. _____

So the prophets spoke out to help people recognize God's action and God's will for them as expressed in the covenant. They spoke out to warn people when they were following the forces of evil and going against God's covenant. They predicted the consequences if the people ignored their warnings and continued to cooperate with the forces of evil by worshiping false gods.

Because it was the Holy Spirit who "spoke through the prophets," what the prophets taught has permanent value. Their words continue to be God's message and continue to have value even today. Their teachings can help us recognize God's presence and action, as well as help us recognize the forces of evil, the lasting effects of original sin, at work in today's society.

POST-IT QUOTE

Therefore, thus says the LORD, assuredly I am going to bring disaster upon them that they cannot escape . . .
Jeremiah 11:11

Scripture Search

The prophet Isaiah was a great religious leader who warned the Hebrews about their wrong-doings and repeatedly reminded them of God's fidelity to them. Read Isaiah 1:16–17.

- According to Isaiah, what does God tell his people to do?

_____

_____

_____

- In what ways are Isaiah's words meaningful today?

_____

_____

_____

In addition, today the Holy Spirit continues to gift people with this special spiritual sensitivity. We have prophets today, too. And they have the same kind of mission as the prophets of old. They speak out and help us recognize the action and presence of God in our midst. They also help us recognize and warn us of the evil forces at work in our society and call us to oppose those evil forces. They speak out against racism, abuse of any sort, greed, oppression of those who are poor, war, and violence. They speak out against those powerful people and institutions that promote injustice. Finally, like the prophets of old, today's prophets make all kinds of enemies who want to silence them.

What's Your View?

Form a group with two or three of your classmates. Share your responses to the following questions.

1. If a prophet like Jeremiah or Isaiah were to come to your community, to what injustices or forces of evil might he or she try to draw people's attention? What techniques would he or she use to reach the people? How would your community respond to him or her?

2. A prophet is, above all, a guide. He or she tries to guide people in making good choices. Who are some of the prophets who speak to young people today?

ON YOUR OWN
Speaking through the Prophets

What individuals or service organizations in your community work against injustice, abuse, violence, or oppression? Your chamber of commerce, your librarian, or even your local telephone directory may give you some leads. Report your findings to the class.

Journey Within

Write about a time when you have acted as a prophet to someone else, perhaps a friend or brother or sister.

_____

_____

The Holy Spirit and you

You received the Holy Spirit of the Father and the Son at your Baptism. From that moment on, the Holy Spirit has lived in you. The Holy Spirit is the all-powerful bond of divine love that unites you with Jesus and God the Father. The Spirit provides the grace for you to respond to the love of Jesus and the Father and to extend that love to all you meet. Yet the Holy Spirit never takes away your free will. You can choose to ignore the Spirit's promptings.

POST-IT QUOTE

Every time we say "I believe in the Holy Spirit," we mean that we believe there is a living God able and willing to enter human personality and change it.
J.B. Phillips

At your Confirmation, the Holy Spirit is poured out upon you in a new and special way, like the oil used in the sacrament. You are anointed by the Spirit. Through this anointing you are empowered, enlightened, and commissioned to go forth like the first apostles to be a messenger, a witness, a herald to all the world. You are sent out to tell all who will listen the good news of God's love and the salvation God offers us through Jesus.

ON YOUR OWN

Preparing for Sharing in the Mission of Jesus

How does your parish help prepare young people to celebrate the Sacrament of Confirmation? Interview your priest or director of religious education to find out if special meetings, projects, or activities are part of the preparation. Report your findings to the class.

If your parish is in the process of preparing a group of young people for Confirmation, offer to be a prayer partner for one of the candidates. As a prayer partner, you make a special effort to pray for the candidate as he or she prepares for the sacrament. You might write notes or letters to the candidate, encouraging him or her during this period of action and reflection. Some prayer partners choose to remain anonymous; others reveal their identity right away or shortly before or after the candidate has been confirmed.

What's Your View?

Form a group with two or three of your classmates. Share your responses to the following:

Confirmation is sometimes called the "Sacrament of Christian maturity" because it completes the initiation into Catholicism begun through Baptism and Eucharist. In your opinion, what characteristics of religious maturity should a young person possess in order to be considered a good candidate for Confirmation?

You will always have the living presence of the Holy Spirit within you. This presence begins at your Baptism and equips and commissions you for ministry through your Confirmation. Actual grace can be received at special times of need or challenge. Sometimes grace helps you help someone else. The Spirit moves you to come to someone's aid or to say just the right words to advise or console a friend. Sometimes grace is just for you, to help you fight off some temptation or to find the courage to challenge some evil.

Catechism Corner

Whether extraordinary or simple and humble, charisms are graces of the Holy Spirit . . . (799)

Journey Within

Write about a time when you helped a friend who was having a difficult time. Did you realize that the Holy Spirit was working through you?

_____

_____

_____

_____

ON YOUR OWN

Listen to the Silence

Find a quiet spot away from the noise of family, friends, and everyday hustle and bustle. Stay there for awhile—fifteen minutes or longer. Listen to the silence. Hear the words the Holy Spirit speaks to you in your heart.

The point is, the Holy Spirit is always active within you, always there to guide, support, console, strengthen, and encourage. In other words, the Holy Spirit is God's constant love—both within you and all around you, like the water that surrounds a fish. You live and move and draw every single breath within the loving presence and grace of the Holy Spirit. That's what we believe when we say the words, "I believe in the Holy Spirit."

The gifts of the Holy Spirit

The gifts of the Holy Spirit are special powers of the Spirit bestowed on the Church and all its members to enable them to carry out Jesus' mission.

Wisdom is the capacity to see with God's eyes. Wisdom helps us see the big picture to enable us to do God's will more perfectly. This gift of the Spirit helps us know the core truths, principles, and values that underlie all of reality.

Understanding is the God-like capacity to see beneath the surface of a problem or an issue and recognize what is really involved. For example, when people say or do cruel things, in most cases, they are not actually cruel people. It takes understanding to realize they may actually be lonely, frightened people who are crying out for help.

Knowledge is the God-like capacity to get the facts straight, to recognize the difference between truth and error.

Right judgment (counsel). Gifted by God's wisdom, understanding, and knowledge, you will be able to figure out how best to act in a tough situation. You will also be able to help others do the same. To have the gift of counsel is to always have God's advice available to you when you need it.

Courage (fortitude). Wisdom, understanding, and knowledge enable you to be convinced with a God-like conviction of what is good. Then you have a God-like strength to be able to hold on to and defend that good no matter how difficult or dangerous it might be to do so.

Reverence (piety). Because you are gifted with God's wisdom, understanding, and knowledge, it will be totally clear to you what it means to be God's beloved child, someone very special to God. And you'll always want to pray and act the way a grateful and loving child would pray and act.

Awe in God's presence (fear of the Lord). Again, gifted with God's wisdom, understanding, and knowledge, you'll have a keen awareness of just how special and awesome God really is. You will know that nothing exists that is more important than God. You would rather cease to exist than deliberately betray God's love for you.

Reflection

A reading from Paul's Letter to the Romans 8:14–16.

For all who are led by the Spirit of God are children of God. For you did not receive a spirit of slavery to fall back into fear, but you have received a spirit of adoption. When we cry, "Abba! Father!" it is that very Spirit bearing witness with our spirit that we are children of God . . .

You are a dwelling place for the Spirit of God. In what ways are you a good dwelling place? How might you improve?

Prayer for Today

Side One: *All-powerful God, Father of our Lord Jesus Christ, send us your Spirit to be our helper and guide.*

Side Two: *Fill us with the spirit of wisdom and understanding so that we might make the complex simple and the unseen visible.*

Side One: *Fill us with the spirit of knowledge and right judgment so that we might recognize what is good and always choose the path that leads to it.*

Side Two: *Fill us with the spirit of courage so that we live our faith without fear or hesitation.*

Side One: *Fill us with the spirit of reverence and awe in your presence so that your glory may shine through us and touch the lives of everyone around us.*

Side Two: *We ask you for these gifts through your Son, Jesus. Amen.*

Team Spirit

God has chosen you to be on his team and gifted you with the Holy Spirit. Design a logo for the hat your team will wear to signify that you have been inspirited. Then develop a team motto and team cheer and choose a mascot.

Team motto: _____

Team spirit cheer: _____

_____

_____

_____

Team mascot: _____

Chapter 6

THE BODY OF CHRIST

. . . the holy catholic Church . . .

Setting the Stage: The Web

How are you "connected" to the other members of your class? What do you have in common? What unites you? This game will help you find out.

Students should form a circle. One student in the circle holds onto the end piece of a ball of yarn and tosses the ball to one of the other members of the group. The first student relates to the group how he or she is "connected" to the second: for example, they share the same first name, are the same height, have the same color eyes, are in the same class, or live on the same street. The second person, keeping hold of the yarn, tosses the ball to a third student in the circle, telling the other players how he or she is connected to that player. The third player selects a fourth, and follows the same routine. The game proceeds in this fashion until all the players have been "connected" to one another in a giant web.

While your web is still intact, think about what else unites you and your classmates in terms of what you are studying in this course.

A lesson in vocabulary

Something you need to remember is this: When the Apostles' Creed was first developed, it wasn't written in English as you read it today. The English words didn't even exist.

The original Creed was written in Greek and then in Latin long before it came to be translated into the English words we now have. So to understand what the words "holy catholic Church" really mean, we first need a vocabulary lesson.

ON YOUR OWN

A Vocabulary Lesson

Match each word with its definition. In the blanks, write the Greek and Old English words (see the list of italicized words) from which the modern English word is derived. (Don't use a dictionary; make educated guesses, if necessary!)

Terms	Greek or Old English word	Definition
___ Ecclesiastical	_____	A. spiritually whole or pure; godly
___ Church	_____	B. "the assembly of the people"
___ Holy	_____	C. comprehensive or universal
___ Catholic	_____	D. an organized religion; a building used for religious purposes

chirche (Old English) *kyriakon* (Greek)

kata (Greek) *halle* (Old English)

holos (Greek) *ekklesia* (Greek)

Prepared by that little vocabulary lesson, we can get a better idea of the meaning of the words "holy catholic Church" that we use today.

When the Apostles' Creed was first developed, our word *church* did not exist. The word that was first used was *ekklesia*, which means "assembly of the people." So our Creed expressed belief in the *ekklesia* or the "assembly of the people." But it wasn't just any assembly of people. The Apostles' Creed refers to that visible assembly of the people who are united to Jesus and one another through Baptism. It is the assembly of the people of God, built by Jesus on the foundation of the apostles and led by the successors of Peter and the apostles.

POST-IT QUOTE ☑

But you are a chosen race, a royal priesthood, a holy nation, God's own people . . .

1 Peter 2:9

Scripture Search

Read Matthew 28:16–20 and John 21:15–17. Both of these passages relate how the risen Jesus sent his apostles to complete his mission on earth in special ways.

1. What were they to teach? To whom?

2. What special sign were they to perform to initiate new disciples?

3. What did Jesus mean when he told Peter, "Feed my sheep"?

4. The leaders of our Church—its bishops and priests—are Peter's successors. According to Jesus, what is their mission?

Because it is the assembly of the people of God, united to Jesus, it is an assembly that has received and is enlivened by the Holy Spirit of Jesus. So it is a *holy*, pure, and God-like assembly. Because the assembly is united to Jesus, *everyone* in the assembly, to the best of his or her ability and with God's grace, accepts and tries to live out everything revealed to us by God through Jesus.

It is a *catholic* assembly that embraces and embodies all that Jesus taught and all that was handed down by the apostles, not just selected parts. Marked by Christ's presence, it is a catholic assembly because it is sent out to the whole world to be a sign of Jesus' gift of redemption to everyone.

Today the word *Church* as used in our Creed has come to mean the same thing as *ekklesia*. It refers to the assembly of the people of God. Keep in mind, however, that our English word *church* has several other meanings as well. It can refer to a building where a religious group gathers, and it can also refer to religious groups in general. (For example, some Churches in the United States are increasing membership.) The word can also refer to one aspect of a religious group, such as its hierarchy, or official leadership. (For example, the Church published a letter to all its members on the issue of abortion.)

It is important to remember that when we express belief in the Church as we pray the Creed, we are referring to the assembly of the people of God.

ON YOUR OWN

Nicene Creed Wording

The Nicene Creed speaks of the "one holy catholic and apostolic Church." These are called the four marks of the Church. Short definitions for three of the words were given earlier. With a partner, research Part One, Section Three, Article 9, paragraph 3, numbers 811 through 870 in the *Catechism of the Catholic Church*. Write your additional understanding for each of the words given based on the information you have read.

- one _____
  _____
  _____

- holy _____
  _____
  _____

- catholic _____
  _____
  _____

- apostolic _____
  _____
  _____

Add your understanding of each word to the list composed by the rest of your classmates.

ON YOUR OWN

Word Power

A popular magazine tells its readers, "It pays to increase your word power." We agree! In the first column below you will find the Latin, Greek, or Old English word from which a modern English word, listed in the second column, is derived. Match the modern English word to its Latin, Greek, or Old English partner. Then match the definitions in the third column with the appropriate modern English word. Do not use a dictionary; rely on knowledge you already possess or make educated guesses.

Latin, Greek or Old English	Modern English	Definitions
___ ___ 1. *presbyteros*	A. lord	A. a humble and sincere request
___ ___ 2. *sacramentum*	B. creator	B. a binding agreement
___ ___ 3. *communio*	C. resurrection	C. a sharing
___ ___ 4. *dominus*	D. priest	D. having unlimited power
___ ___ 5. *precaria*	E. almighty	E. ruler; master
___ ___ 6. *covenire*	F. creed	F. one who creates
___ ___ 7. *credere*	G. prayer	G. visible sign of a hidden reality
___ ___ 8. *apostello*	H. father	H. an elder
___ ___ 9. *resurrectus*	I communion	I. to trust; to believe
___ ___ 10. *pater*	J. covenant	J. a rising from the dead
___ ___ 11. *ealmihtig*	K. sacrament	K. male parent
___ ___ 12. *creator*	L. apostle	L. person sent forth on a mission

What's Your View?

Form a group with two or three of your classmates. Share your responses to the following questions.

1. In your opinion, what meaning do most Catholic Christians associate with the word *church*? Support your answer with examples.

2. For many adults, "being a good Catholic" means going to Mass on the weekend, saying bedtime prayers, abstaining from meat on Fridays during Lent, and sending their children to a Catholic school. Is there more to being a good adult Catholic? Explain your response.

3. What do we mean when we say we—the people of God—are a *visible* assembly? Is it important for us to be visible? Explain your answer.

Breakaway

The People of God

The Catholic Church is often understood as a hierarchy. Imagine a pyramid divided into five segments, with the pope at the top, the bishops beneath him, the priests and deacons beneath the bishops, other professed religious beneath the priests, and the laity on the bottom. Many ordinary people, members of the laity, felt they had a very small role—if any—in the Church.

The Church's leaders who met during the Second Vatican Council (1962–65) wanted to balance this picture of power. They wanted to emphasize the oneness of the Church and the importance of each of its members.

It takes participation by all in the decision-making and work of an organization for a sense of unity and oneness to develop and for the organization to succeed and continue.

Imagine that the Church is a sports team, orchestra, business, or some other structure or organization. With two or three of your classmates, develop a graphic (a picture, drawing, chart, diagram) that demonstrates what position each person or group mentioned in the first paragraph above would play in the organization you have chosen. Clearly state how decisions would be made and what kind of work each person or group would have to do for the organization to succeed. How is the Church working toward the goals of unity and oneness?

Present your work to the class.

A divine reality, a human institution

To believe in the Church is to admit that we're involved in a mystery. The Church is God's doing. It has a divine origin and quality.

Catechism Corner

The Church is both the means and the goal of God's plan . . . (778)

The Church is a community of people who, because of their union with Jesus, are the visible extension of Jesus. To be Church is to be the body of Christ present on earth today, continuing to carry out the mission of Jesus. Ultimately, the Church cannot fail to fulfill the mission given it by God. It has the power to forgive sins in God's name, to teach and heal in Jesus' name, to be a sacrament of salvation, and to bestow the Holy Spirit.

What's Your View?

Get together with a partner. Share your ideas about the Church's mission. What do we mean when we say we are the "visible extension" of Jesus?

On the other hand, the Church is also a human institution made up of human beings like you and me who can err, who can sin, who can make a mess of things and fail miserably. As a human institution, the Church can get caught up in politics and the struggle for power. It can be greedy, cruel, deceptive, and indifferent to the needs of those who are poor and oppressed. And if you know your history, the Church *as a human institution* has been all those things at various times, starting way back in the time of the apostles. Just read Paul's First Letter to the Corinthians, for example.

Scripture Search

Saint Paul, one of the Church's first missionaries, established a Christian community in Corinth. This city was well known for the immoral behavior of many of its citizens. Occasionally Paul heard reports that the Christian community was not living as it should. Read 1 Corinthians, chapter 5, and then respond to the questions that follow.

1. In your own words, summarize this passage.

2. What are some of the behaviors of the Corinthians that Paul condemns?

3. Paul commands the Corinthians to make of themselves "fresh dough." What do you think he means by this? What is the new "yeast" he refers to that will help the Corinthians become renewed?

4. If Paul wrote a letter to your neighborhood or community, what would he tell its residents about how they should live?

ON YOUR OWN

It's a Good Thing

How is your parish helping to meet the needs of those who are poor? Interview your pastor or another parish leader to find out. Report what you learn to the class.

Volunteer your services to an organization in your parish or community that serves the needs of those who are poor. For example, you might work for an afternoon at your community's food pantry or shelter for those who are homeless.

So when you say you believe in the holy catholic Church, you believe that this assembly of people really is the body of Christ visible on earth, possessing the divine qualities and power of Jesus—even though as a human institution it also has all the flaws of any human institution. That the Church can be both divine and human is a central part of the mystery we embrace when we say we believe in the holy catholic Church. Let's look at this idea in a little more depth.

Keeping your focus

At the human level, the Church is an assembly of recovering sinners. At its human level, it will have flaws until the very end of time. At the same time, the Church remains a community of saints, the body of Christ, holy and sinless, acting in Christ's name to forgive and to make holy, acting to heal and guide.

Catechism Corner

The Church is the Body of Christ. . . . In the unity of this Body, there is a diversity of members and functions. All members are linked to one another, especially to those who are suffering, to the poor and persecuted. (805–6)

Some people make the mistake of just focusing on the human and flawed part of the Church. Perhaps they complain that the members seem to be hypocrites, or that the leaders seem to be out of touch with the times, or that the Mass is boring and poorly celebrated. By focusing only on the Church's human flaws, people get discouraged. Sometimes they end up using these flaws as an excuse to drop out of the Church altogether.

ON YOUR OWN

Drop Out or Cop Out?

Young people sometimes focus only on the flaws of the school system they attend as an excuse to drop out: "The teachers are too strict"; "The classes are boring"; "The other kids don't accept me." If a student drops out, he or she misses many opportunities. Make a list of ten opportunities a drop-out misses. Compare your list to a classmate's.

- If a person decides to "drop out" of the Church, what opportunities does he or she miss?

It's important that you keep your focus. You don't have to pretend the Church doesn't have flaws because it does—at the human level. What you need to learn to do is look beyond this human level to the holiness and power of Jesus that the Church also possesses. That's where faith comes in.

A good example is your weekend Eucharist. If you focused just on how the Eucharist is celebrated at the human level, it could seem like a disaster. Here's a "worst-case" scenario. The priest is tired or crabby and acts that way. Most of the people seem disinterested, and the singing sounds that way. The lector proclaims the readings in an annoying nasal twang. The server is a nine-year-old who fidgets all the time and distracts everyone. The Eucharistic minister is a known alcoholic. We're exaggerating, of course, but you get the point.

But this same Eucharist is still an action of the body of Christ. Even though the priest has human flaws, Jesus is still present, offering a perfect sacrifice of worship to the Father. With faith, you'll believe this. Even though the lector has an annoying voice, God's word is still proclaimed, giving life and guidance to the assembly. Even though the server is in constant motion, the Holy Spirit still descends upon the gifts of bread and wine on the altar and transforms them into the Body and Blood of Christ. You can "see" this through faith. Even though the Eucharistic minister has a drinking problem, you can still receive Christ from his or her hands. And even though you may hardly know the people around you, you are united to them at a deeper, spiritual level in the assembly and in the sharing of the Body and Blood of Christ. You'll experience this kind of communion because of your faith.

POST-IT QUOTE

. . . all of you are one in Christ Jesus.
Galatians 3:28

Scripture Search

Paul tried to teach members of the Christian community at Corinth how they were all united despite their many differences. Read 1 Corinthians 12:12–30. Respond to the questions that follow.

1. Give a brief summary of this passage.

2. According to Paul, how have all the different people who live in Corinth been united?

3. What comparison does Paul make to help the Corinthians understand that they are all members of the Church, the body of Christ?

4. According to Paul, how should the members of the Church in Corinth act toward each other? Why?

ON YOUR OWN

He's Only Human

How well do you know your parish priest? Is he just a distant figure dressed in unusual clothing you see at Mass on the weekend—something not quite human? It may surprise you to know just how human he is. Interview your priest: learn about his family background, his childhood experiences, his education, and how he chose his vocation. He may also be willing to tell you about his hopes, fears, dreams, strengths, and weaknesses.

Write a biographical sketch about your pastor. Perhaps your work can be published in the parish bulletin or given to new parishioners to help acquaint them with your priest.

Be sure to use good communication skills in arranging and conducting your interview. This includes writing a thank-you note to your priest after the interview is concluded, and allowing him to preview your work before it is made available to a wider audience.

The Church is the body of Christ, even if this body is made up of flawed and sinful humans like you and me. It is precisely by being a member of the body of Christ that we flawed and sinful people become a people transformed into Christ. So if you want the fullness of holiness, truth, and happiness that comes from being a member of the body of Christ, you are going to have to get used to being part of a flawed and sinful people. And then, through faith and grace, you will be able to discover and experience how the Holy Spirit is constantly acting to transform this flawed and sinful people (including you) more and more completely into the body of Christ, filled with his holiness and truth. Your faith will keep things in focus.

Breakaway
A People Transformed

Complete this project with two or three of your classmates. From a large piece of construction paper or poster board, cut out a human silhouette. Illustrate one side of this figure with signs, symbols, and expressions of our flaws and sinfulness as humans. Illustrate the other side with signs, symbols, and expressions of how as members of the Church we are transformed into the body of Christ. Present your work to the class.

Belonging is a gift

A good song has the same basic effect on its listeners. Everyone who hears it gets caught up in its rhythm and the mood it creates, and they can identify with the message it communicates. A good song that is well sung makes everyone feel good. It can turn a group of strangers into a community, at least for a few moments.

Breakaway
Top Ten and More

Form a group with three or four of your classmates to complete the following activities.

1. Make your personal "top ten" list. Rank your ten all-time favorite songs in the blanks below. Be able to explain why you chose the songs you did. Compare your list with those of the other members of your group.

   Number 1 _____

   Number 2 _____

   Number 3 _____

   Number 4 _____

   Number 5 _____

   Number 6 _____

   Number 7 _____

   Number 8 _____

   Number 9 _____

   Number 10 _____

2. Identify five occasions when a group of people sing together and form a community, even if only temporarily.

   _____

   _____

3. Your group is in charge of selecting the music for a special teen Mass. The theme for this celebration is "We Are Friends in Jesus." You may select any music you wish, as long as it is appropriate to the theme of friendship. What songs would your group choose for each part of the liturgy?

   _____

   _____

4. Think of a song that makes you feel good. Sing it or play it for your group in such a way that they will get caught up in the music!

Here's a kind of comparison. Think of the message of redemption and fullness of life that God seeks to share with all humanity as a song. God wants everyone to hear and get caught up in this song. Now think of the Church as a special choral group God has formed to sing this song of redemption so that everyone will hear it and eventually get caught up in it. Being chosen as a member of this special choral group (the Church) is a gift you have received.

Journey Within

Write a thank-you letter to God for his gift of choosing you to be a member of the Church.

_____

_____

_____

_____

Maybe the comparison seems a little strained, but it is true that, as a member of the Church, you have been personally picked by Jesus to be a part of the group who are to bring the message of God's reign to all the world.

POST-IT QUOTE

Go therefore and make disciples of all nations . . .
Matthew 28:19

Being a part of this select group doesn't make you better than those to whom you are sent. (Remember, the Church is still a group of recovering sinners.) But being part of this select group does put you in a better position to come to know and understand just what it is God intends for all humanity.

Being a member of the Church means you already have access to the fullness of truth all people long to discover. You can already experience a closeness or intimacy with God in the sacraments that many people do not yet know is even possible for them. In short, being baptized into the Church is a very special gift!

The mission of the Church: a promise and a proof

God ultimately intends that all humanity be united to him. That's what God promises to bring about despite our tendency toward sinfulness and selfishness. This promise began to be revealed to the children of Abraham and was renewed throughout the Old Testament. This promise is made loudly and clearly by Jesus, and is contained in his teaching about the nature and the coming of God's reign.

The Church of Jesus' followers is the visible beginning of the fulfillment of God's promise. The Church is men and women united to Jesus, filled with his Spirit, transformed into the body of Christ. The Church is a visible proof that what God has promised is, in fact, possible. God keeps his promises! Just as important, the Church is a kind of preview of the reign of God proclaimed by Jesus. The Church reveals what the reign of God will be like when it is established in its fullness at the end of time.

POST-IT QUOTE

For the kingdom of God is . . . righteousness and peace and joy in the Holy Spirit.
Romans 14:17

This is what the mission of the Church is all about: to tell all people about the redemption and the reign of God that Jesus has established; to be a visible, living sign of this reign of God, which will be fulfilled at the end of time, and thus to be visible, living proof that God can and does keep his promises.

How do we, the Church, go about this mission? We do it by striving to live out the gospel message in our everyday lives: by forgiving each other, caring for each other, sharing with one another, reaching out to the people who are poor, hurt, and oppressed by unjust rulers or institutions. Most simply, we do it by striving to do and say what Jesus did and said. To the degree that we do this together, we will be fulfilling our mission as Church. We will be showing people what God promises, and we will be giving proof that God is keeping that promise.

What's Your View?

How can you live the gospel in your everyday life? To whom can you offer forgiveness? How can you show a caring attitude toward your family, friends, and the environment? With whom can you share more generously? How can you reach out in a small way to those who are hurting because of the unkind or unjust actions of others?

The Catholic Church

For almost one thousand years, there was only one Church, and that Church was catholic. (The word *catholic* means "universal.") That Church and everyone in it embraced the revealed truth of God that was taught by Jesus. The pope (the bishop of Rome and the successor of the apostle Peter, whom Jesus appointed head of the Church) was considered by everyone to be its head. During that first thousand years, it wasn't necessary to talk about the Catholic Church as distinct from any other Church. There was simply "the Church."

Scripture Search

Read Matthew 16:13–20. This passage tells how Jesus gave Peter a special mission. Use what you learn from your reading to fill in the crossword puzzle.

Across

4. Another name by which Peter is known.
5. Peter tells Jesus he is the _____.
7. Jesus tells Peter, "My _____ _____ revealed this to you.
8. Peter tells Jesus he is the Son of the _____ _____.
9. "You are _____, and on this _____ I will build my church. . . ."

Down

1. This is the "neighborhood" where these events take place.
2. Jesus asks, "Who do people say that the _____ _____ _____ is?"
3. His disciples told Jesus some thought he was John, the _____.
6. Jesus entrusted the _____ to the kingdom of heaven to Peter.

There arose a major disagreement between the part of the Church centered in what had been the eastern section of the Roman Empire—called Byzantium—and that part of the Church centered in Rome and the western section of the Roman Empire where the pope resided. Some of the disagreement was over what Jesus had actually taught, but a big part of the disagreement was political.

ON YOUR OWN

East vs. West

Using an historical or religious atlas, locate the areas referred to in the preceding paragraph. Find Rome, the capital of the western Roman Empire. Identify and locate the city that was the capital of Byzantium. What modern-day countries comprise ancient Byzantium? What modern-day city has its roots in the capital of the Byzantine Empire? Share your findings with the class.

The Church had become closely connected with the governments in both the eastern and western parts of the old Roman Empire. The government in the eastern part of the Church and the government in the western (Roman) part of the Church were at odds. In the process, the eastern part of the Church rejected the primary or head leadership of the pope and affirmed its own leadership. In 1054 C.E., there arose an eastern Church (mostly what we today call *Orthodox*) and a western Church (mostly called *Catholic* today.) This break became known as the *Great Schism* (split), and the schism remains to this day, even though there has been much reconciliation and healing recently.

Catechism Corner

The *Pope*, Bishop of Rome and Peter's successor, "is the perpetual and visible source and foundation of the unity both of the bishops and of the whole company of the faithful." (LG 23.) (882)

ON YOUR OWN

Check It Out

Research some of the beliefs held by Orthodox Christians. Your librarian or director of religious education can help you locate resources for your work. Share what you learn with the class.

In the sixteenth century, there was a new challenge to the Catholic Church. Martin Luther began a movement that became known as the *Protestant Reformation*. He and several others disagreed with some of the teachings and practices in the Church, saying the Church had strayed from Jesus' original teachings. These reformers also disagreed with the belief that the pope had the authority of Saint Peter as head of the Church. Various kings and princes, eager to get rid of the political power of the pope and the Roman Empire, sided with these reformers.

As a result, many new Christian Churches came into existence, each claiming to be the real Church. Each had some different ideas about what Jesus actually taught, but they all agreed on one thing. They would not accept the pope as the successor of Peter and as head of the Church Jesus founded.

Today we have many different Christian Churches, each claiming to possess the fullness of the truth taught by Jesus. But some basic differences divide them. Besides rejecting the authority of the pope, some Churches do not share the Catholic Church's beliefs about the nature and meaning of the sacraments, the nature of the priesthood, and even some aspects of the nature of redemption itself.

However, because our Catholic Church and the various reformed or new Christian Churches all believe in Jesus and in the Scriptures, the members of other Christian Churches are considered our brothers and sisters in Christ. In the years surrounding the millennium, special efforts are being made by the Catholic Church and other Christian Churches to come to greater understanding regarding the areas that previously separated them.

ON YOUR OWN

Brothers and Sisters in Jesus

Make a list of the different Christian Churches in your community and their religious affiliations. (The yellow pages of your telephone directory will be helpful.) Interview a representative from one of these Churches to find out what beliefs about God, Jesus Christ, and the Holy Spirit you share. Report what you learn to the class.

So today, to be a Catholic means that you believe the Church is founded on the apostles and continues, through the leadership of the pope and the bishops, to encourage others to embrace and spread the good news about God and God's kingdom as taught by Jesus.

What's Your View?

Form a group with two or three of your classmates. Share your responses to the following questions.

1. In your opinion, why do the various Christian Churches often seem to focus more strongly on the beliefs that divide them rather than the beliefs that unite them? Explain your answer.

2. In your opinion, what action might the leaders of the Catholic Church take to help bring about Church unity? What might your parish family do to help bring about that unity among the Churches in your community?

In this short chapter, we have only been able to hit the most basic truths of what we believe when we say, "I (We) believe in the holy catholic Church." We haven't talked about how Jesus continues to lead and guide the Church through the pope and bishops, for example. We haven't talked about the special role the sacraments play in the life of the Church. So what you've read in this chapter are the basics that have been handed down since the very beginning of the Church. You can see that the short statement of belief—"I believe in the holy catholic Church"—is truly rich in meaning.

Reflection

In John 17:20–23, Jesus prayed to his Father in these words.

"I ask not only on behalf of these, but also on behalf of those who will believe in me through their word, that they may all be one. As you, Father, are in me and I am in you, may they also be in us, so that the world may believe that you have sent me. The glory that you have given me I have given them, so that they may be one, as we are one, I in them and you in me, that they may become completely one, so that the world may know that you have sent me and have loved them even as you have loved me."

Jesus has many disciples today whose words and actions carry on the mission of the apostles. Who are the people in your life who have led you to Jesus, and through Jesus to God the Father?

Many people argue that they don't have to belong to the Church to be good persons and relate to God. They say they can do this on their own. Do you agree or disagree with their ideas? Explain your answer.

Prayer for Today

Dear Jesus,

We come before you as members of your Church, your body, the people of God. We are grateful for the special gifts that this membership brings.

Help us look beyond the human flaws of our Church to the holiness and power it possesses through your Spirit.

Help our Church leaders shepherd us with justice, compassion, and love.

Lead us to greater unity with our sisters and brothers of other Churches.

Help us see clearly the goals you have set before us, and give us the strength and courage we need to carry out our mission of bringing the good news of salvation to all people everywhere. Amen.

HOMEWORK

Early Christians used a number of different symbols or "codes" to communicate to each other that they were followers of Jesus—members of the Church. One of these symbols was the fish, which represented Jesus Christ. Design a symbol that represents the one holy catholic Church of the twenty-first century.

Chapter 7

SAINTS AND SINNERS

. . . the communion of saints, the forgiveness of sins . . .

Setting the Stage: Helter Shelter

How good are you at creating order out of chaos? Form a team with two or three of your classmates. Using only a stack of old newspapers and some masking tape, create a shelter that will house your small group comfortably. When it is completed, test its durability. Compare your shelter to those constructed by other groups. Did working with your classmates make the task easier or more difficult? Why?

Cooperation

Did you ever watch *Mister Rogers' Neighborhood* when you were a preschooler? If you did, you'll be familiar with the word *cooperation*. Mr. Rogers always stressed to his young audience the importance of cooperation. And for good reason, too. To cooperate literally means "to work together." That is a good description of a fundamental law of our entire universe: things working together. The earth and the sun work together to make life on earth possible. All forms of life on earth work together in ecosystems. Each single living thing requires constant cooperation within itself among all its cells and organs. The more complex the life form, the greater the cooperation.

Breakaway

Over, Under, and Through

This challenge requires lots of cooperation. (Not to mention flexibility!) Get together with six or seven of your classmates. Stand in a circle, side by side, with everyone facing the inside of the circle. Reach toward the center of the circle and join hands with two people not standing next to you. Without letting go of hands, untangle the human knot you have formed by stepping over, under, and through each other's arms. Your goal is to get everybody untwisted and end with a circle in which everybody is holding hands with the people on either side of them. Can you do it?

POST-IT QUOTE

Human beings are social creatures. We are affected by the presence of people around us. You see the ball game better at home on television, but you experience the ball game better if you go out to the stadium. It's a hard thing to find God by yourself.
Rabbi Harold Kushner

The same rule applies to society, too. No social group—from the smallest family to the largest nation—can survive if its members don't work together. Nations must cooperate with nations not just to maintain peace but to be able to provide to the entire human family essentials such as food, shelter, medical care, and education.

What's Your View?

Form a group with two or three of your classmates. Choose one of the following situations to think about. Share your conclusions with the class.

1. Last night for supper you had a hamburger from your favorite fast-food restaurant. Trace the life of that burger from the cow to your stomach in terms of the cooperation that had to occur to get it there. See if your group can list at least ten "cooperative efforts."

2. Think about your family's daily routine in getting ready for work and school. How do members of your family cooperate during the morning rush? What improvements might be made through increased cooperation?

3. Occasionally a labor organization will call a strike. The chain of cooperation temporarily breaks. What results (good and bad) from this break in cooperation? Who is affected? In what ways?

As Christians, we believe this fundamental law of cooperation goes beyond the physical and social order. It extends to the spiritual order as well. When we say we believe in the communion of saints, the spiritual order is what we are referring to.

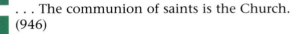

Catechism Corner

. . . The communion of saints is the Church. (946)

Our first Christian ancestors certainly believed this. They felt it was important enough to be included in our list of fundamental beliefs. They felt it was critical to understanding and living the Christian life. So we need to form a clear idea of just what this communion of saints actually is.

In the early Church

In the early Church when our Creed first developed, in various places for nearly three hundred years there were terrible persecutions against Jesus' followers. No one knows the exact numbers, but it is generally agreed that many, many Christians were killed during that period. Just about every living Christian knew someone—perhaps a relative or a friend—who died in these persecutions. If they didn't know anyone personally, they were familiar with the stories of the many heroic women and men who bravely endured torture and faced death rather than deny Jesus.

Scripture Search

Read the biblical account of the death of the first Christian martyr, Stephen, in Acts 7:54–60. Write a news article about his murder. Remember the five "W"s journalists keep in mind: who, what, when, where, and why. Share your work with the class.

Saul of Tarsus, who was an enthusiastic persecutor of the new Christians, had been present at Stephen's murder. But Saul became one of the Church's most extraordinary missionaries after his conversion to the Christian faith. Read Acts 8:1–3 and 9:1–22 to find out how this transformation occurred. Then complete the crossword puzzle.

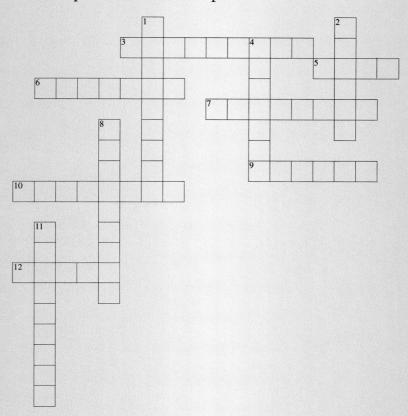

Across

3. How long Saul's affliction lasted

5. Saul's other name (see Acts 13:9)

6. Who Saul proved Jesus was

7. People to whom God would send Saul

9. What the Lord said Saul would have to do in his name

10. City to which Saul was traveling

12. This came from the sky

Down

1. Question Saul asked the voice

2. Something similar to these fell from Saul's eyes

4. Disciple who baptized Saul

8. "Why do you _____ me?"

11. Saul's affliction

Our ancestors in faith also knew that their martyred friends and relatives were now in heaven with Jesus. Because they had been bound together so closely on earth through their common faith, their friendship, and their love for Jesus, it was natural enough to believe this spiritual bond continued beyond death.

This means that their martyred loved ones who were now with Jesus could continue to help and support them—the living—if they asked them. So our ancestors began to pray to God through these Christians who had died. Their prayers were often quickly rewarded, sometimes in miraculous ways. More often their prayers were answered in unseen, spiritual ways that were just as real.

Catechism Corner

". . . we believe that in this communion, the merciful love of God and his saints is always [attentive] to our prayers" (Paul VI, CPG § 30). (962)

Through their prayers to their martyred friends and relatives, our ancestors felt themselves able to grow in their ability to understand and live the gospel and in their willingness to share with and to help one another.

The early Church had no trouble believing there was a powerful spiritual link between themselves and those who had died in faith. They believed the Christians on earth and their friends who were in heaven were still in communion—united together. Their loved ones in heaven could continue to help those on earth. They could cooperate—work together—with those on earth.

Journey Within

You may be familiar with Granddad, one of the characters Bil Keane created for his comic panel "The Family Circus." Granddad, even though he is deceased, is very much "alive" to his family in their thoughts and memories. Write about one of your loved ones in heaven who is very much alive in your thoughts and memories. Have you ever felt that person's spiritual help?

_____

_____

_____

_____

_____

A word about saints

In the phrase *communion of saints*, the word *saint* does not have that very specialized meaning we usually give the word today when we talk about the saints in the Church. In the Creed, the word *saint* refers to all people, both on earth and in heaven, who are united to Jesus. Those in heaven are united to Jesus "face to face." People like us who are on earth are united to Jesus through faith and Christian living.

ON YOUR OWN

Face to Face

Make a list of your family members and friends who are now saints united face to face with Jesus. Record their names and the dates of their birth into eternal life below. A parent, guardian, or other family member might help you complete this project.

Name	Birth into eternal life
_____	_____
_____	_____
_____	_____
_____	_____

Regardless of how one is united to Jesus, it is the bond with Jesus, the sharing in Jesus' own Spirit and holiness, that makes a person a saint. So, as the word *saint* is used in our Creed, it means that anyone united to Jesus, whether in heaven or on earth, qualifies as a saint. To say you believe in the communion of saints is to say you believe that all those united to Jesus, both on earth and in heaven, are saints.

What's Your View?

Get together with a partner. Share your ideas about what we mean by the word *saints* in the phrase "communion of saints."

ON YOUR OWN

Ordinary People

Use the phrase *communion of saints* to form an acrostic that communicates the idea that saints are ordinary people. In the spaces provided, write the names of saints whose name begins with each of the letters. Remember the definition of a saint given above: a saint is anyone who is united to Jesus, whether in heaven or on earth. In order to balance your list with names of both the living and the dead, you may want to search in various books on the lives of saints for names of saints who are in heaven. Display your choices for others to view.

C _____

O _____

M _____

M _____

U _____

N _____

I _____

O _____

N _____

O _____

F _____

S _____

A _____

I _____

N _____

T _____

S _____

The Church's understanding grows

The real question is this: Who is united to Jesus and thus qualifies as a saint? The early Church focused on its living members and its dead Christian friends and relatives, especially the martyrs, when it thought about who was united to Jesus. But over the centuries, the Church began to expand its understanding of sainthood and thus expanded its idea of just who should be included in this communion of saints.

The Church realized that throughout history there have been many people, like the ancient Hebrews, who never had a chance to know about Jesus or to become members of the Church. But as the Church pondered the Scriptures and the teachings of Jesus, it came to realize that through God's mercy these people could experience the redemption God offered through Jesus.

This certainly included Abraham and Sarah, Jacob and Rebecca, Amos, Isaiah, and other well-known Old Testament people. The communion of saints also includes all those who seek God with a sincere heart and who, through God's grace, try to live a morally good life.

Catechism Corner

. . . Because he was "strong in his faith," Abraham became the "father of all who believe." (*Rom* 4:11, 18; 4:20; cf. *Gen* 15:5.) (146)

What's Your View?

Get together with a partner. Share your ideas about how the Church's understanding of the "communion of saints" expanded.

And grows

The Scriptures make it clear that God's redemption is made available to all people in all times. Anyone who has accepted this redemption gained by Jesus is welcomed into heaven at death and is united to Jesus.

So the understanding of the communion of saints has grown since the days of the early Church. It includes more than martyred friends and relatives. We now believe it includes all those united to Jesus in heaven and on earth. Because you are united to Jesus in faith, you are also in communion with all those in heaven.

The Church also believes that some people, though they die in God's grace and are redeemed by Jesus, do not enter immediately into heaven. They must spend some time in a state or condition the Church calls *purgatory*, where they must atone for past sins before they can enter heaven. They, too, are members of the communion of saints.

Catechism Corner

All who die in God's grace and friendship, but still imperfectly purified, are indeed assured of their eternal salvation; but after death they undergo purification, so as to achieve the holiness necessary to enter the joy of heaven. (1030)

ON YOUR OWN

A Friend in Need

As a member of the communion of saints, you are a friend to all the souls in purgatory. Your prayers can help them. Tonight say a special prayer for one of these friends in need.

Finally, there is one other dimension to this communion of saints you are called to believe in. This spiritual bond, this "working together," isn't just a link that ties those on earth with those in heaven and purgatory. It also ties together—into communion—all those on earth who are united to Jesus. At this minute, you are united by spiritual bonds to all Christians all over the world.

Breakaway

It's a Small World after All

Form a team with several of your classmates. Create a symbol for the unity of all Christians worldwide through their membership in the communion of saints. Volunteer your symbol for the cover of your parish bulletin or newsletter.

Getting practical

Talking about spiritual ties with people in heaven or with people on the other side of the world can seem pretty vague and abstract. (Spiritual realities seem like that when you are first learning about them.) What is so important about this communion of saints that it is included in our Creed?

Go back to the idea of working together. Our earliest ancestors believed—really believed—that their friends and relatives who were in heaven could continue to help them, as they did when they were on earth. And they could! That's basically what the communion of saints meant for them. Over the centuries, we've expanded the idea of who is in this communion of saints. But the basic truth—that those in heaven with whom we are united can help us—remains the same.

Do you realize how many people in heaven are praying for you? They are both able and eager to help you, just as the early martyrs helped our Christian ancestors. All you need to do is believe, as your Christian ancestors did, that they can and will help you. On the practical level, then, to believe in the communion of saints is to believe the saints in heaven have power to help you here on earth, and then, through prayer, to ask for that help.

Journey Within

Write about a problem you faced recently for which you found a good solution. Do you think you might have had help from an unexpected source?

_____
_____
_____
_____
_____

We're not talking magic, of course. Praying to the saints to help you pass a test when you didn't study for it isn't going to work. But you can be sure of this. If you want help in being a good person, if you want help in dealing with the problems and weaknesses you experience, if you want help in growing in courage and generosity and faith, you can get all the help you need by asking your allies in heaven to pray for you. You can count on them every bit as much as you now count on your friends on earth. That's what being a member of the communion of saints is really all about—helping each other.

Make a list of three of your closest friends. In what ways can you count on them? How do they count on you?

Name of Friend	How I count on her/him	How she/he counts on me
_____	_____	_____
_____	_____	_____
_____	_____	_____

What's Your View?

Form a group with two or three of your classmates. Share your responses to the following questions.

1. What qualities do you value most highly in a friend? Give examples to support your choices.

2. What events or circumstances are most likely to cause a friendship to end? Do these same threats to friendship exist in your relationships with your allies in heaven? Explain your answer.

3. "Yeah, I've tried praying to my so-called 'friends' in heaven," your neighbor tells you. "It didn't work. I told them I wanted my mom to buy me these really cool jeans at the mall. Instead I had to get a cheaper pair that was on sale because they're last year's style. Praying didn't do me a whole lot of good!" How would you respond?

Not just in heaven

It's the same with your bond to all the other Christians now on earth. You can draw strength from their example, their suffering, their courage, their holiness. And you can be a source of strength for them, too, simply by your own efforts to be a friend of Jesus and follow his gospel message. Because we believe in the communion of saints, we know there is a spiritual link between us and all other Christians. We can communicate spiritual energy, help, and strength to each other— including those in purgatory—even though we can't see it happening. We are working together!

Again, you do this especially by praying. By the prayers and the sacrifices you offer, you can obtain God's help for friends, for relatives, for people on the other side of the world you don't even know, and for those in purgatory. That's one of the reasons we have the general intercessions at each Eucharist. In the same way, others are helping you with their prayers and sacrifices. That is the communion of saints in action, and that's what you believe when you say, "I believe in the communion of saints."

We celebrate All Saints' Day on November 1 each year. Applying what you have learned about the communion of saints in this chapter, write the general intercessions to be offered during the liturgy for that holy day.

1. _____
_____

2. _____
_____

3 _____
_____

4. _____
_____

5. _____
_____

The forgiveness of sins

Why do you suppose our ancestors put "forgiveness of sins" right after "communion of saints" in our Creed? At first, it would seem that there is no connection between the two beliefs. To help see this connection, you need to remember that you were probably born into a Catholic family and are being raised a Catholic. Unlike you, many of the first Christians were adults who had been converted from a pre-Christian lifestyle, which was very different from how the gospel teaches us to live. Their conversion was often a very powerful experience. (Remember Saul's story?) They became deeply convinced of the sinfulness of their past lives and regretted that sinfulness very deeply. To them, a major part of their experience of conversion centered on how generous and merciful God was to have forgiven them. They also realized that it was through Jesus' willingness to die for them that this forgiveness was given to them.

So for the early Christians, to enter the Church, to become a saint and a member of the communion of saints was closely linked to the experience of God's forgiveness of their sins. The forgiveness of their sins was a central part of what they experienced and thus had come to believe as Christians. Their Baptism, which marked their conversion, was the celebration of this forgiveness. It united them to Christ and gave them the Holy Spirit, just as the Sacrament of Baptism does for new Christians today.

What's Your View?

Get together with a partner. Share your ideas about why belief in the forgiveness of sins is closely connected to the belief in the communion of saints.

Just as important, our ancestors were professing belief that this forgiveness is available over and over. It isn't offered just once, at the time of one's conversion. Their experience told them that it was all too easy to slip back into sinful actions and habits, even after being converted. If forgiveness were available only once, most people would be in big trouble.

POST-IT QUOTE

If we say that we have no sin, we deceive ourselves, and the truth is not in us.

1 John 1:8

Remember how we described the Church as a community of recovering sinners? Well, God's forgiveness is what makes that recovery possible. It is what makes the Church possible. Because God's forgiveness is always available, even if people fall back into their old life of sin, God's forgiveness continues to sustain the Church.

Scripture Search

A famous story of forgiveness that Jesus told his disciples is found in Luke 15:11–24. Read the story and then rewrite it with modern characters and settings. With a group of your classmates, act out the story for the class.

Catechism Corner

There is no offense, however serious, that the Church cannot forgive. . . . Christ who died for all men desires that in his Church the gates of forgiveness should always be open to anyone who turns away from sin. (Cf. *Mt* 18:21–2.) (982)

So, by including in the Creed the belief in the reality of forgiveness of their own sins, our ancestors were telling the world that this forgiveness is necessary, possible, and available to everyone as often as we need it. The very fact that we have three sacraments that forgive sins—Eucharist, the Sacrament of Anointing, and especially the Sacrament of Reconciliation—indicates the importance that the Church places on this fundamental belief stated so simply in our Creed.

It works both ways

If we are sustained as a communion of saints because of God's forgiveness, two other truths must follow. First, we must be willing to forgive one another.

POST-IT QUOTE ☑

Put away from you all bitterness and wrath and anger and wrangling and slander, together with all malice, and be kind to one another, tenderhearted, forgiving one another, as God in Christ has forgiven you.
Ephesians 4:31–32

Forgiveness is a very special form of love. When a community is made up of weak humans like ourselves, forgiveness is one of the most basic forms our love needs to take. No human community—from the smallest family to the largest nation—can exist very long if there is no willingness to forgive each other. This is also true of that part of the communion of saints that is here on earth. Forgiving others is one of the things you do as a member of the communion of saints. This includes atoning for the sins of others by your good works and sacrifices.

Journey Within

Write about a time when a family member or friend hurt you deeply. Have you forgiven him or her?

_____

_____

_____

_____

Second, because you are united to all others in the communion of saints, there is no such thing as a "private" sin. Whenever you do something sinful, the whole communion of saints on earth is affected. Your sin, no matter how secret it may seem, is like a spiritual virus that infects and weakens the whole community. Arguments like "what I do is my own business" really don't hold water when it comes to doing sinful things. Because you are a member of the communion of saints, what you do is the business of everyone you are in communion with. If your good actions benefit everyone, it follows that your evil actions affect everyone, too.

POST-IT QUOTE ☑

There's a ripple effect
In all that we do;
What you do touches me;
What I do touches you.

Breakaway

Ripple Effects

When we drop a pebble into the water, ripples radiate outward. One small action can have far-reaching effects. The same is true of our daily actions. Our wrongdoings have ripple effects, hurting other members of the communion of saints. Similarly, our sacrifices and good deeds have a positive impact on those whose lives touch ours through a shared union with Jesus.

Get together with a partner. Select two or three scenarios from the list below. Discuss with your partner how the action described in the scenario might impact others in the communion of saints.

- damaging school property
- volunteering to do a chore for an elderly person
- regularly taking small amounts of money from your mother's purse
- giving money to charity rather than spending it on yourself
- lying to your parents
- fighting at home or at school
- shoplifting from a large department store
- giving up an afternoon with your friends to visit your grandfather, who is in a care center
- cheating on a test
- picking up cans, papers, and other litter in your neighborhood
- making fun of someone in your class who is "different"
- returning some money you found in a store to the manager
- inviting an unpopular classmate to be part of your group for a school project
- spending Sunday afternoon studying when all of your friends are at the mall
- convincing someone to do something for you that might get him or her into trouble
- not complaining when you learn you have to share your bedroom with a younger sister or brother

Canonization

The process through which a person becomes officially recognized as a saint by the Church is called *canonization*. This term comes from the Greek word *canon*, which means "rule" or "list." To be canonized is to have your name added to the official list of saints.

In the early Church, there was no formal canonization process. Anyone martyred for their faith was considered a saint, and all the Church honored the martyr as such. In time, the persecutions ended and martyrdom became uncommon. Then the Church simply proclaimed certain persons saints if they had the reputation among the people for having lived a holy life. But there was no special process for this.

By the Middle Ages, however, the Church began to develop a more formal process for determining who should be enrolled in the official list or canon of saints. There are now three steps to canonization.

First, a person's cause or case must be introduced. Anyone may introduce a person's cause. The Congregation of Rites investigates the person's life to see if the person displayed a heroic degree of holiness during his or her life. If the decision is positive, the person is then called "Venerable."

A second, more rigorous investigation is begun. This investigation examines every known detail of the person's life, the person's writings, and any miracles attributed to the person. An official biography must be written. If sufficient holiness is demonstrated, the pope declares the person "Blessed." He or she can be honored by the local Church where the person lived or by the religious community to which he or she may have belonged.

A third and final step now begins. The person's life is thoroughly reexamined. This evaluation includes reasons why the person might not actually be worthy of sainthood.

During this investigation, at least two officially-recognized miracles must ordinarily be proven to have taken place because of the intercession of the blessed person.

If no obstacle is found and the miracles are proven, the pope then declares the person a saint and enrolls her or him in the official canon or list of saints. A feast day is appointed (if not done earlier), and the whole Church is encouraged to honor and pray for the intercession of the new saint.

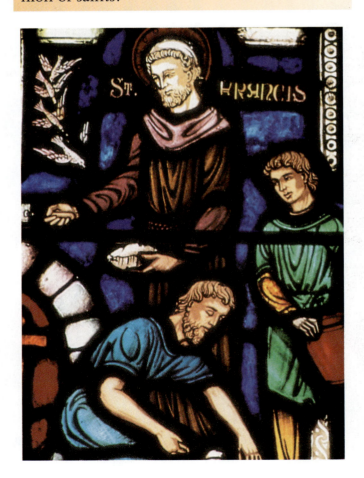

ON YOUR OWN

Honor Roll

Select five of the holy people listed here and research their lives. Try to find the dates each reached the various stages of canonization. (Your librarian, teacher, or director of religious education can help you locate resources.) Also, identify the day of the year each one is honored. Share your findings with the class.

Saint Francis Xavier Cabrini

Saint Elizabeth Ann Seton

Saint Maximilian Kölbe

Saint Anthony of Padua

Saint Maria Goretti

Venerable Pierre Toussaint

Saints Joachim and Anne

Saint Vincent de Paul

Saint Elizabeth of Hungary

Blessed Kateri Tekakwitha

Saint Nicholas

Saint John Neumann

Venerable Catherine McAuley

Saint Martin de Porres

Because the canonization process is now long and complex (even when a person is considered a martyr [for example, Archbishop Oscar Romero] or recognized by many as a very holy person [for example, Mother Teresa]), raising persons to sainthood is not nearly as common as it was in the early Church. This doesn't mean we don't have as many saints as in earlier times. It just means the Church is now more selective about whom it holds up to the entire Church as a person worthy of honor and imitation.

What's Your View?

Form a group with three or four of your classmates. Share your responses to the following questions.

1. In your opinion, which step of the canonization process is most demanding? Explain your answer.

2. Do you think the canonization process is too long and complex? Defend your answer.

3. In your opinion, which twentieth-century figures are excellent candidates for canonization? Why?

Reflection

For I know my transgressions,
*   and my sin is ever before me.*
Against you, you alone, have I sinned,
*   and done what is evil in your sight,*
so that you are justified in your sentence
*   and blameless when you pass judgment.*

Restore to me the joy of your salvation,
*   and sustain in me a willing spirit.*
Then I will teach transgressors your ways,
*   and sinners will return to you.*
Deliver me from bloodshed, O God,
O God of my salvation,
*   and my tongue will sing aloud of your deliverance.*
*   —Psalm 51:3–4, 12–14*

Whose forgiveness do you need to seek?

How will you atone for your wrongdoing?

Prayer for Today

Side 1: *We are saints.*

Side 2: *We are united to Jesus. Because he has redeemed us, we are gifted with sainthood.*

Side 1: *In our sainthood, we are united with our brothers and sisters throughout the world who hear God's word and keep it.*

Side 2: *In our sainthood, we are united with all our brothers and sisters throughout the ages: those who came before us and those who will come after us.*

Side 1: *Jesus, help us be deserving of our sainthood. Open our hearts to your love so that, through us, it can embrace others.*

Side 2: *Help us joyfully forgive those who hurt us just as you have forgiven us.*

Side 1: *Help us follow your example and choose to do what is good, what will bring us closer to you.*

Side 2: *We are saints, Jesus. Help us remember that. Amen.*

"There are different gifts, but the same Spirit," wrote Paul to the Corinthians. (See 2 Corinthians 12:4–12.) With what talents has the Holy Spirit gifted you? How can you use these talents for the good of the communion of saints? Write your answers here.

Create a symbol for three of your talents. Then tell how you can use each talent to bring honor to the Church, the body of Christ.

Chapter 8

FROM HERE TO ETERNITY

. . . the resurrection of the body and life everlasting. Amen.

Setting the Stage: In Memory

All of us will someday end our earthly life-journey. How do you wish to be remembered by your family, friends, and acquaintances? Use the questions below to focus your thoughts. Then design a memorial to yourself that conveys how you wish to be remembered.

• For what three accomplishments do you want to be remembered?

• What three values do you want your life to have exemplified?

• Who has taught you something that you would like to pass on to others?

• How do you want to have made a difference in the lives of others?

This much is certain

Everyone dies. This is an effect of original sin. Naturally, no one enjoys dwelling on that fact. But from the dawn of human history, the awareness that we are mortal has prompted each new generation to ask what may be the most basic of all religious questions: Does some form of life continue for us after we cease to be alive here on earth? How you answer that question determines how you view the meaning of human life.

Journey Within

Write about your first experience with death. What were your thoughts? How did you feel? What questions did you have? Were you satisfied with the answers you were given?

_____

_____

_____

_____

It seems that lower life-forms can't ask why they exist. Driven by natural instinct, they simply spend all their time and energy doing two things: trying to provide for their basic needs (food and safety) and trying to propagate and protect their offspring so that their species will continue to exist.

If we were like these lower life-forms and death ended our existence, those would be the only two purposes of our existence, too: doing our best to enjoy the short life we have and trying to ensure that we will have offspring who can keep the species going. Unlike lower life-forms, however, we are not driven by blind instinct. We can choose to focus entirely on our own pleasure and happiness, even if it means ultimately destroying our species—and ourselves. Abortion, drug abuse, violence, and the exploitation of our environment are sad examples of this.

What's Your View?

Form a group with three or four of your classmates. Share your responses to the following questions.

1. Discussing death makes many people uncomfortable. In your opinion, why is this so?

2. If it were within your power to live an earthly existence forever, would you choose to do so? Why or why not?

3. What evidence do we have today that many people focus entirely on their own pleasure and happiness?

A universal dream

It seems that as a species we have never been satisfied with the idea that everything ends with death. Deep in our being is the desire to be immortal. Deep in our being is the hope that life, in some form or another, does continue for us after our short time here on earth.

We find in the most ancient gravesites of our primitive ancestors, for example, tools and stores of food intended to help the dead person in that mysterious life after death. Also, the worship of the spirits of ancestors (which presumes they continue to exist) is one of the oldest forms of religion.

ON YOUR OWN

If You Could Take It with You . . .

In ancient cultures, people were often buried with possessions that were intended to ease their journey through the afterlife. If you could take three of your possessions with you beyond death, what would they be? Why would you choose these?

97

So it is safe to say that, throughout our human history, we have never been content to presume that death is the end of our existence. Ideas about what that post-death existence might be like are as varied as the religions we have developed that seek to explain why we exist. For example, the Hindu religion—one of the oldest in the world—teaches a belief in reincarnation. To state simply what is actually a highly-developed and complex religious belief, one can say that Hindus believe that, after death, people keep being reborn in new life forms until they are "perfected."

The religions of the ancient Egyptians, Greeks, and Romans—in fact, the religions of almost all the ancient civilizations—taught belief in some form of afterlife. In most instances, it was not a very good existence, except for the select few whom the gods chose to join them in a kind of paradise. It was usually believed that most of the dead remained in a kind of shadowy underworld. This was not a place of great pain or of great pleasure, but it was better than nothing.

ON YOUR OWN

Journey Beyond Death

Research the beliefs of the ancient Egyptians regarding death and its aftermath. You might wish to explore information about the pyramids that housed the burial chambers of Egypt's rulers and the mummification process that helped preserve the bodies of these people. Share your findings with the class.

POST-IT QUOTE

Death, thou shalt die.
John Donne

We are an Easter people

What is unique in our faith isn't the idea of "life after death." It is the nature of this life. In our Creed, our Christian ancestors are quite clear on what we believe. We believe in "the resurrection of the body" as well as "life everlasting." The faith of our ancestors, the first Christians, literally began with the experience of the resurrection of Jesus. We are disciples of the risen Lord!

At the very foundation of our faith, then, is the belief that Jesus has conquered death. More than that, like Jesus, we, too, will experience a resurrection of our body after our death. United to Christ in life, through the work of the Holy Trinity we will be united to Christ—body and spirit—in a glorified and glorious life after death. We are an Easter people.

POST-IT QUOTE

I am not dying; I am entering life.
Saint Thérèse of Lisieux

What's Your View?

Get together with a partner. Share your ideas about why we Christians are an Easter people.

The experience of the risen Jesus altered history forever. It transformed what was a general idea and a religious hope into one of the most basic beliefs of our faith. This belief is unique in all of human history.

Catechism Corner

. . . Just as Christ is risen and lives for ever, so all of us will rise at the last day. (1016)

Not just a "near-death" experience

There are many stories, all well-documented, of people who "died" from one cause or another (accident, operation, severe illness) and who came back to life. These people underwent an "out-of-body" experience, and then were revived. If you read the resurrection accounts in the four Gospels, however, it is clear that Jesus did not have just a near-death experience. Nor was he simply revived. He truly died and was buried. When he reappeared on that first Easter, his body had experienced a radical transformation. It no longer had any of the physical limitations of a physical body.

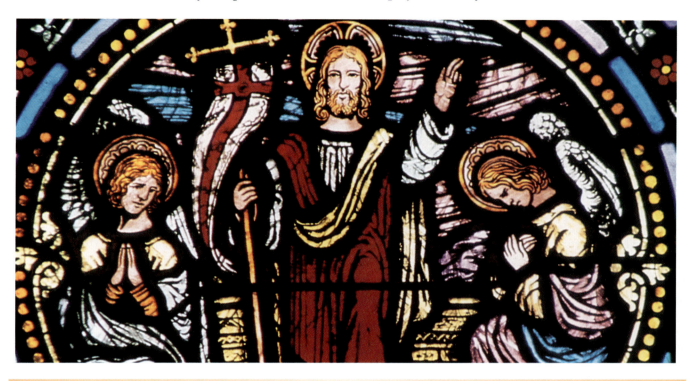

Scripture Search

Read the Gospel accounts listed below, which tell about the activities and characteristics of the risen Jesus. What did Jesus do that proved he was still human? What did he do that showed he had been physically transformed? Complete the chart.

Scripture references	The human Jesus	The spiritual Jesus
Matthew 28:1–10		
Luke 24:13–35		
John 20:11–18		
John 20:19–29		
John 21:1–14		
Acts 1:1–11		

We can't really explain it because we have nothing with which to compare it. But after God the Father raised Jesus, his body had all the qualities and capacities we usually associate with a spirit. He wasn't subject to the physical laws of time and space. He could appear and disappear at will. He could pass through closed doors.

But Jesus wasn't a ghost, either. The apostles could see and touch him. They could talk to him. Jesus even ate with them. In the Gospel accounts, it's very clear that the apostles weren't describing some ghostly appearance. It was Jesus, in the flesh. It's also clear that the body of the risen Jesus had been transformed and given spiritual powers it did not have before his death.

So when our Creed says we believe in the "resurrection of the body," it is stating the belief that all of us will experience this same kind of resurrection and spiritual transformation of our own bodies at the end of time. Your body will be perfect, beautiful, glorious, beyond all suffering, sickness, pain, or need. Whatever physical limitations or defects you may experience on earth (poor eyesight or lameness, for example) will end. Yet—and this is what is difficult to imagine—you will be the same person you are right now.

What's Your View?

Form a group with two or three of your classmates. Share your responses to the following questions.

1. Who are our models of physical "perfection" today? How is working to be like a model of physical perfection beneficial to a young person? How can it be damaging?

2. In your opinion, what might be God's idea of a body that is physically perfect?

POST-IT QUOTE ✓

"What no eye has seen, nor ear heard, nor the human heart conceived, what God has prepared for those who love him.". . .

1 Corinthians 2:9

Life everlasting

It's hard for us to comprehend what the words *life everlasting* actually mean. As humans, we are locked into thinking in terms of segments of time: minutes, hours, days, and years. We always think in terms of "before" and "after," and "past," "present," and "future." We remember the past, live in the present, and dream about the future. It's just about impossible not to think like that.

Journey Within

Revisit your past and travel to your future. Write a paragraph that describes the "you" of two or three years ago. Then write a paragraph that describes the "you" you would like to be at age twenty-five.

_____

_____

_____

_____

_____

But after death, we pass out of time as ordinarily defined. We will exist in an ever-present *now*. The entire past will be present in that now. The entire future will be present in that now. Time, as we know it, simply won't exist! Do you see why it's so hard to imagine what "life everlasting" will be like?

Every once in a while, we do get little glimpses of what it might be like, though. Everyone has some experience of when time seems not to exist. Maybe you were at Disney World or skiing or swimming or on vacation or at a party or family gathering. You got so caught up in the fun and happiness of that experience that you lost all sense of time. When the happy time finally did end, you probably thought, "Where did the time go?" And you meant it. During that all-absorbing, joy-filled experience, time ceased to exist for you.

Well, that kind of experience can help you get some idea of what the experience of "life everlasting" will be like. It will be an all-absorbing present. You will be so absorbed in the now that you feel no need or desire to worry about the past or the future.

So, contrary to what some people fear, "life everlasting" won't be boring. Being bored is related to the experience of time and the yearning for something more perfect. You're bored when time seems to pass slowly and nothing seems to be happening. But in "life everlasting," time doesn't pass slowly—because there is no time as we know it. In "life everlasting," everything is happening right now. To put it simply, in "life everlasting" you won't have time to be bored!

 What's Your View?

Form a group with two or three of your classmates. Share your responses to the following items.

1. Tell your group about a great experience you had when you lost all sense of time.

2. What is the most perfect, wonderful, joy-filled, pleasure-filled, peace-filled earthly experience you can imagine? How do you think this experience compares with heaven?

3. The mystery of heaven is beyond our ability to understand and describe. The Scriptures use images like *light, life, peace, wedding feast, the Father's house, banquet,* and *paradise* to describe heaven. What image(s) would you choose to help someone understand what heaven is like?

Good news, bad news

At our death, our lives will be judged on how well we have loved. When Christ returns in glory at the end of time, there will be a last judgment when all will rise and all we have done—good or bad—and all we have failed to do, will be revealed. At that time, where we spend our "life everlasting" will be made known to us.

Just as we can't fully imagine what it will be like to exist without time as we know it, it is impossible to imagine the fullness of joy, peace, and happiness that awaits us in heaven. Our most perfect and satisfying experiences as humans don't begin to come close to the experience of sublime happiness that awaits the redeemed. That's the good news.

But don't forget this: Because we are truly free, it is possible to spend "life everlasting" separated from God, totally entrapped in one's own selfishness, totally frustrated spiritually and physically, totally absorbed by hatred of God, of others, and of oneself. That's hell. And hell is real! It is possible for people to spend their lives in total selfishness, choosing to think only of themselves, while disregarding God and others.

Although God is always willing to forgive, some people may never ask for God's forgiveness. They can choose to die in their selfishness. If that is how some people live and how they choose to die, then that is how they will spend their "life everlasting."

 POST-IT QUOTE ✓

I believe it is God's desire that everyone would be saved, that everyone would know the love of God. But I think that God has given us such freedom that we actually can say "no" to him and he respects even our "no."

Dr. Roberta Hestenes

What's Your View? 👁

Form a group with two or three of your classmates. Share your responses to the following questions.

1. The Catholic Church teaches that hell is a place or state of eternal punishment for sin. When you were a child, what images or ideas did you associate with hell? Have your ideas about hell changed? Explain your response.

2. People sometimes refer to a difficult life experience as a "hell on earth." What do they mean?

Hell is not some fable made up to scare children into being good. It is mentioned often in both the Old and New Testaments. It also makes sense based on human reason. If we humans have free will—and we do—then we can choose to reject God. God desires us all to spend eternal life with him. Yet, God gives us a free will with which we can choose to reject him. To make that choice in this life means that such a person will spend life everlasting rejecting God. And that's hell!

Is anyone actually in hell? To be honest, we simply don't know. The Church firmly believes and teaches that hell is a reality. The Church firmly believes and teaches that hell is always a possibility for a human with free will. But the Church has never stated that anyone actually is in hell. Why? Because how God applies infinite justice and infinite mercy to any individual—even the most public and unrepentant sinner—is God's secret. It is not our place to know or judge another's sins or God's mercy.

Scripture Search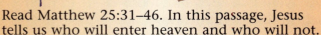

Read Matthew 25:31–46. In this passage, Jesus tells us who will enter heaven and who will not.

- What actions does Jesus encourage us to perform in order to spend life everlasting with him? List specific examples that promote these actions in today's world.

Catechism Corner

. . . The chief punishment of hell is eternal separation from God, in whom alone man can possess the life and happiness for which he was created and for which he longs. (1035)

Here and now

Our Creed is clear on this much: you will experience a resurrection of your body at the end of time when Christ comes again in glory. You are going to continue to experience life everlasting in that resurrected body. That's what our faith tells us will happen. But what difference does this make for you right here, right now? Well, to begin with, when the full meaning of this belief really sinks in, you should view your present life with new eyes.

As an old commercial said (though for entirely different reasons), "You only go around once." God has called you into existence so that you can grow into a loving, generous, caring, joy-filled person—*now*. Every day is an important opportunity to grow. Every decision is an important opportunity to grow. You have only so many days, so many opportunities to grow. How you use them determines the kind of person you will be for all eternity.

ON YOUR OWN

A Little Math

If you live to be seventy-five years old, how many hours will you have available to you for deciding what kind of person you will be for all eternity?

Catechism Corner

. . . Our lives are measured by time, in the course of which we change, grow old and, as with all living beings on earth, death seems like the normal end of life. That aspect of death lends urgency to our lives: remembering our mortality helps us realize that we have only a limited time in which to bring our lives to fulfillment. . . . (1007)

POST-IT QUOTE

God created people so that we would create the one thing in the world that God could not create by himself, and that is the choice of goodness.
Rabbi Harold Kushner

Another effect of believing in life everlasting is that you begin to view your body with new eyes, too. Your body is you. You are destined to spend all eternity in bodily form. Your body isn't something extra added on to you, like a set of clothes. You will spend eternity as an embodied person, a unity of body and spirit. The body that's going to be transformed at your resurrection is the body you have right now. You've often been told that you are precious and irreplaceable in the eyes of God. Well, this precious, irreplaceable you that God loves is the embodied you. Scripture describes your body as a temple, a scared creation intended to give honor and glory to God. Showing reverence for your body and caring for it here on earth is, in a real sense, a religious act, a religious duty.

Breakaway

Body Talk

Form a team with three or four of your classmates. Develop a list of at least ten tips for maintaining a healthy body. Your list may include advice about diet, exercise, sleep, drug use/abuse, or any other wellness factor. (Your teacher may suggest resources you can use in completing this phase of your project.)

Create a chart, poster, or collage to illustrate your tips. Post your work in the classroom or hallway.

Finally, because of your belief in resurrection and life everlasting, you begin to view death with new eyes. When you realize you are going to live forever, you see death as only one moment of transition poised between time and eternity.

POST-IT QUOTE

Death is no more than passing from one room into another.
Helen Keller

This doesn't mean that death is insignificant. Because you are made for life, you will always instinctively fear and rebel at the natural level at the idea of dying. At this level, Jesus himself feared and rebelled against the idea of dying.

But when you believe in life everlasting, you can face the idea of dying with peace and confidence as Jesus did. As Paul wrote when talking about the life everlasting Jesus has won for us: "Where, O death, is your victory? Where, O death, is your sting?" (1 Corinthians 15:55) So those two phrases in our Creed— "the resurrection of the body" and "life everlasting"—aren't just high-sounding words to file away in your memory. They are deeply meaningful truths to live by.

ON YOUR OWN

Lifeline

Create a poster that features your lifeline: a chronological summary of your growth toward fullness of life as a loving, generous, caring, joy-filled person. On your lifeline, record the dates of your birth, Baptism, First Communion, along with any other oppor-tunities for growth in your faith that occurred during your childhood. Reserve one segment of your lifeline for the present. What are you doing now to become the person God intends you to be?

As you move into the future (which should also be a part of your lifeline), what opportunities for positive growth do you anticipate? What choices and decisions can you make as a high school student and as an adult that will lead to life everlasting?

Finally, create a symbol that expresses your transition from mortal life to eternal life. What kind of heaven do you believe awaits you?

"Amen"

If you've ever attended or watched on television a prayer meeting or a "revival meeting," you may have heard the word "Amen!" shouted often, loudly, and with great conviction by the believers present. This is the way "Amen!" is intended to be said.

Catechism Corner

In Hebrew, amen comes from the same root as the word "believe." This root expresses solidity, trustworthiness, faithfulness. . . . (1062)

You see, *amen* is a Hebrew word that is a kind of oath. It can be translated in various ways such as, "You can bet your life that's true!" Or, "I agree with you to the very depths of my heart." Or, "I swear to God this is true." If this is what *amen* really means, then you can see why it deserves to be shouted out, to be said with great feeling, real conviction, and gusto.

ON YOUR OWN

I Couldn't Have Said It Better Myself

List three expressions we use today to communicate the same conviction that "Amen!" conveys.

To mumble "Amen" so that it can hardly be heard or to sort of grunt it out so a listener can't even understand the word takes away its real meaning. Saying "Amen" without enthusiasm or feeling is about as convincing as the husband who mumbles, "Of course I love you" to his wife while he is totally absorbed in reading his newspaper or watching a football game on TV.

Breakaway

You Can Say That Again!

Get together with a partner. Brainstorm a list of five statements you consider to be the most important an individual will utter in his or her lifetime. Practice saying these statements to each other the way you believe they ought to be said. (It's okay to laugh a bit during this activity!) If you and your partner are feeling courageous, perform for the class.

Anytime the Church gathers to pray, the congregation is invited to add its "Amen" to whatever prayers are said by the leader. We even have what we call the "Great Amen," with which we conclude the Eucharistic Prayer. Perhaps because of embarrassment or some misguided idea of what is proper, many Catholics tend to say their "Amen"s quietly, without enthusiasm or conviction. They don't give the word the emphasis it deserves.

Sometimes an accompanying gesture helps us give a word or a statement the emphasis it deserves. For example, a "How do you do?" with a handshake communicates an enthusiasm that "Hi there" (with hands in pockets) does not.

With two or three of your classmates, suggest several gestures that we might use during the Great Amen to help lend enthusiasm to our response.

So when you see "Amen" at the end of the Creed, remember what it stands for. Even when you say the Creed (or any other prayer) alone and silently, let that "Amen" at the end remind you of what your attitude should be toward what you just prayed. At least in your heart, let a loud, joyous, enthusiastic "I really mean it and believe it!" ring out. And the next time you celebrate the Eucharist and you are invited to join in the Great Amen at the end of our greatest prayer—the Eucharistic Prayer—try making it a great "Amen." Amen!

Your journey through the Creed is complete. You now have in your hands the same map for life that our ancestors in faith developed and used to guide them. You now know—and hopefully understand—the same basic truths needed to guide you through life.

You know that our God is Father, Creator of heaven and earth. You know that Jesus is God's only Son, both divine and human, born of Mary by the power of the Holy Spirit. You know that Jesus suffered and died to redeem us; that Jesus rose from death, has been raised up to sit at the right hand of the Father, and will come again as Judge at the end of time. You know that the Spirit of God, one with and equal to the Father and Son, actively assists you and the Church.

You know that the Church is the body of Christ, a community of disciples of Jesus who continue to spread the good news of salvation and carry out the work of Jesus here on earth. You know that you are united to the whole communion of saints, all those who accept Jesus' redemption. Finally, you know where it all ends, with the resurrection of your body and life everlasting with God, Christ, the Holy Spirit, and the whole communion of saints.

Much of what you learn in school you remember just long enough to be able to pass a test. Then you either forget it altogether or file it away in your memory for possible use at some later time. Learning about our Creed should be different. You don't learn about it to pass a test and then forget it. You don't learn about it because it may be useful at some later time. All the truths in the Creed are intended to guide, help, encourage, and strengthen you every day of your life, in all your decisions and choices. The Creed gives you "words to live by" right here, right now.

There's one more thing. Before you began this course, you probably already had heard much about the Creed. What we talked about wasn't totally new to you. But, hopefully, you have come to see much of it in a new way and understand and make better sense of it now.

If that was your experience, you can count on the fact that you'll be able to keep gaining new insights into the real meaning of these truths all through your life. Learning about your faith isn't the same as learning a historical fact, a math formula, or a law of science. You can always probe more deeply into the meaning of these truths of our faith. So this shouldn't be the end of your study of the Creed. In a real sense, it is just the beginning.

POST-IT QUOTE ☑

Truth is not something finished, but something unfolding as life goes forward.

Rufus M. Jones

Reflection

"I am the resurrection and the life. Those who believe in me, even though they die, will live, and everyone who lives and believes in me will never die." (John 11:25–26)

Read the account of the raising of Lazarus in John 11.
- Who was Lazarus?
- Why did Jesus raise him from death?
- What meaning does Lazarus's story have for Christians today?

Prayer for Today

O Almighty God, we have gathered here to praise and thank you.

We have learned more about you, your Son Jesus, and the Holy Spirit.

We have learned more about our faith and how we are one with you and with each other.

When we say the words of the Creed, help us feel their meaning in our hearts.

Help us understand the message of the Creed as it is proclaimed by your Church.

Most of all, help us live the spirit of the Creed in our actions.

We ask you for your blessing, O God, through Jesus, your Son and our Savior.

Amen.

APPENDIX: YOUR CATHOLIC HERITAGE

Sign of the Cross

In the name of the Father,
and of the Son,
and of the Holy Spirit.
Amen.

The Lord's Prayer

Our Father, who art in heaven,
hallowed be your name;
your kingdom come;
your will be done on earth
as it is in heaven.
Give us this day our daily bread;
and forgive us our trespasses
as we forgive those
who trespass against us;
and lead us not into temptation,
but deliver us from evil. Amen.

Hail Mary

Hail, Mary, full of grace,
the Lord is with you!
Blessed are you among women,
and blessed is the fruit of your womb, Jesus.
Holy Mary, Mother of God,
pray for us sinners,
now and at the hour of our death.
Amen.

Trinity Prayer

Glory to the Father,
and to the Son,
and to the Holy Spirit.
As it was in the beginning, is now,
and will be forever. Amen.

Prayer to the Holy Spirit

Come, Holy Spirit, fill the hearts of your faithful,
And kindle in them the fire of your love.
Send forth your Spirit and they shall be created.
And you shall renew the face of the earth.
Lord, by the light of the Holy Spirit
you have taught the hearts of your faithful.
In the same Spirit
help us relish what is right
and always rejoice in your consolation.
We ask this through Christ our Lord. Amen.

The Jesus Prayer

Lord Jesus Christ,
Son of God,
have mercy on me, a sinner.
Amen.

Gifts of the Holy Spirit

Wisdom

Understanding

Right judgment (Counsel)

Courage (Fortitude)

Knowledge

Reverence (Piety)

Wonder and Awe (Fear of the Lord)

Fruits of the Spirit

Charity	Generosity
Joy	Gentleness
Peace	Faithfulness
Patience	Modesty
Kindness	Self-control
Goodness	Chastity

Nicene Creed

We believe in one God,
the Father, the Almighty,
maker of heaven and earth,
of all that is seen and unseen.
We believe in one Lord, Jesus Christ,
the only Son of God,
eternally begotten of the Father,
God from God, Light from Light,
true God from true God,
begotten, not made, one in Being with the
    Father.
Through him all things were made.
For us men and for our salvation
he came down from heaven:
by the power of the Holy Spirit
he was born of the Virgin Mary, and became
    man.
For our sake he was crucified under Pontius
    Pilate;
he suffered, died, and was buried.
On the third day he rose again
in fulfillment of the Scriptures;
he ascended into heaven
and is seated at the right hand of the Father.
He will come again in glory
    to judge the living and the dead,
and his kingdom will have no end.
We believe in the Holy Spirit, the Lord, the
    giver of life,
who proceeds from the Father and the Son.
With the Father and the Son he is
    worshiped and glorified.
He has spoken through the prophets.
We believe in one holy catholic and
    apostolic Church.
We acknowledge one baptism for the
    forgiveness of sins.
We look for the resurrection of the dead,
and the life of the world to come. Amen

The Beatitudes

Blessed are the poor in spirit,
    for theirs is the kingdom of heaven.
Blessed are they who mourn,
    for they will be comforted.
Blessed are the meek,
    for they shall inherit the land.
Blessed are they who hunger and thirst for
    righteousness,
    for they will be satisfied.
Blessed are the merciful,
    for they will be shown mercy.
Blessed are the clean of heart,
    for they will see God.
Blessed are the peacemakers,
    for they will be called children of God.
Blessed are they who are persecuted for the sake of
    righteousness,
    for theirs is the kingdom of heaven.

The Ten Commandments

1. I am the LORD your God. You shall not have strange gods before me.
2. You shall not take the name of the LORD your God in vain.
3. Remember to keep holy the LORD's day.
4. Honor your father and your mother.
5. You shall not kill.
6. You shall not commit adultery.
7. You shall not steal.
8. You shall not bear false witness against your neighbor.
9. You shall not covet your neighbor's wife.
10. You shall not covet your neighbor's goods.